The Rugged Road To Recovery

Post Depression Era

Phyllis Bigelow

Eloquent Books
New York, New York

Eloquent Books
An imprint of AEG Publishing Group
845 Third Avenue, 6th Floor - 6016
New York, NY 10022
www.eloquentbooks.com

ISBN: 978-1-60860-104-2

Printed in the United States of America

Book Design: Stacie Tingen

Dedication

To my loving children

Dennis, Vicki, Kimberlee,
Bradley, Michelle, and Melanie

and

sweet grandchildren

Chad, John, Peter,
Amy, Jenny, Adam,
Colin, Aaron, Shane,
Erica and Kyle

Authors Note

After telling my children stories of my life as a child and those of my family, some have encouraged me to write a book of these stories. I do so in love and appreciation of who my children are. I am ever grateful for each of them coming into my life and expect that one day we will be all living a life of pure bliss together forever!

It is my hope that telling my stories will help my children and grand-children better understand who I am and why. For others, I desire them to gain insight into the effects of the environment upon humans. My genuine longing is that my collection of stories be read by today's youth and all those struggling along the rugged road to recovery or in pursuit of living a responsible life.

It is my prayer that perusal of this book acts as a catalyst in promoting new inspiration, motivation, intention and perseverance of the best kind in enhancing the life of each reader. The purpose of my book is to dem-onstrate that overcoming even seemingly insurmountable adversities is an achievable truth as long as intention exists. Perseverance then becomes an indelible etching in the psyche and prevails.

I remain ever grateful to my noble and caring parents for their mani-festation of overcoming obstacles. It resulted in empirical understanding for their children.

Phyllis K Bigelow 2008

Prologue

The stories of a family in RUGGED ROAD TO RECOVERY take center stage around the parents being married in June of 1930 following the onslaught of the great depression of October 29, 1929. The impact of the post depression era upon their lives and the lives of their children is clearly depicted. It becomes not only profound, but far from ephemeral!

A tiny two bedroom farm house built for very temporary living remained the family abode far more years than ever imagined. It came to house seven residents. It never had an ice box. Ice cubes were a luxury never enjoyed in this house. For years it had no electricity. It never had running water and, consequently no bathroom. The outhouse has a seat with two holes and space for outdated catalogs whose pages are used for purposes far from their original intent. The miserable , but necessary little building is a very cold little place in winter and the offensive odor unpleasant in the summer bringing fast exits of its occupants. The parents struggle to try to meet their financial obligations. The farm is not free of financial encumbrance with a possibility of losing it.

Both the blessings and perils of farm life for this family come to life as the stories of this book unfold. They range from humorous to frightening and sad. Though the children's mother had been reared in a quiet, proper and pleasant home with her parents and one sibling, a male four years her senior, she is a patient, kind, calm and caring mother responsible for care of several little children at one time. A matriarch, her children understand her rules are to be honored and she respected. She is a wise, practical, reliable and true lady with admirable morals. Her children know she greatly loves them as it is exhibited by her kind and gentle demeanor. They deeply love her.

She often sings hymns as she works. It may be for creating a sacred atmosphere for her children or for her sanity as simply an uplifting diversion from her daily cares. It is likely that both apply. Soon after marriage her husband makes it clear he holds a misanthropic attitude towards his church which stems from him being ousted from membership for hunting rabbits on Sunday afternoons. The dismissal occurs shortly before his marriage. Knowing the Bible quite well, he has no hesitation to state his case to pastors and others who attempt to get him back in the church.

He finally develops negative ideations about organized religion in general. He insists that his attending church makes him a hypocrite. His view is to his wife's chagrin. When she married him she had believed he was a devout Christian. She does not compromise her beliefs. She is not a nagging wife, and never contradicts him in public.

Being of Irish blood, her husband is an overtly emotional man. He deals with his children much differently than the children's mother. Since he was thirty-one when his first child was born it is reasonable that he may not have the inclination nor patience to be closely involved with them .His wife seems to accept that. He and the mother use bread and milk poultices for soaking an infected foot that contains a sliver .They both check complaints of sore throats and treat them. He does care about his children. The children's father refers to them as their little brood in an affectionate demeanor. He overtly displays moments of affection in various ways. They enjoy his humor. His children know he loves them. His frustration is as quickly displayed as his affection. He reacts rather than responds in a controlled manner which is much different than their mother deals with their children. Where she remains calm, he doesn't. He means well, but just is not well controlled. His wife never disagrees with him in the children's presence. The children love him, but in a different way from their mother.

Poignant revelations of sacrifice, long days of hard work and continual perseverance of their parents are clearly demonstrated in caring for their children and overcoming obstacles. It proves to their children that with intention to overcome adversities that positive results will prevail. The attitude and work ethic of the parents is empirical and becomes instilled in their children. It builds character. The children find it only natural that they help their parents in daily chores as soon as they are old enough to do them. They are aware there is not much money for toys and other things they would appreciate. Few complaints are heard from them or the parents as they pull together in pursuing a better lifestyle.

Chapter 1

About My Parents

My parents married in the year following the onslaught of The Great Depression of 1929. My father was born in June of 1900, thirty when he married eight months into the throes of the depression. He farmed the land he was buying.

With my mother's birthday in December, 1908 she lacked a half year from being twenty-three. She just finished teaching her third year of school a few days prior to their wedding date.

My parents began married life together on a one hundred acre farm my father was buying. It was located about four miles from Ithaca, Michigan in Gratiot County.

My father was reared less than two miles from where my parents now lived. He lived with his parents and two siblings. He had a brother and a sister, both younger than he. His father was a farmer and made his living on a one hundred acre farm.

My father attended rural school through the eighth grade and graduated from Ithaca High School. His report cards reveal a very bright and dedicated student. While in high school, my father learned to play the alto and soprano saxophones. After graduating, he became a member of the local community band and remained a member for many years.

My parents met following a concert where both his brother and my father played. After the concert was over and being a polite lady, my mother congratulated some of the musicians on a wonderful concert. She was aware of eye contact that took place between my father and her. She made it a point to congratulate my father personally. Their first date ensued within a week.

American history greatly intrigued my father. The Civil War was of special interest throughout his lifetime. Over the years, he expressed his views about how the war was handled to anyone who showed interest in listening. It seems natural that both parents found interest in each other early on because of their shared knowledge and interest in history and many other things. They were well-matched intellectually. My father greatly enjoyed taking part in political debates. He was a staunch Democrat and served on the county election board for years. Current historical and political events were very important to my father. He kept well abreast of local, state and national events by radio and newspaper. He always seemed thrilled to tell others that his grandfather had spoken with President Lincoln and they shared a handshake.

Fishing and hunting for sport and food were activities of his expertise and participation. He nearly always was successful in acquiring his prey. He had an ardent desire for listening to professional baseball games, but didn't often have the opportunity so kept track of the plays and scores by news reports from the radio. I remember his great excitement as he listened to the World Series as he sat near his battery run floor radio. Sometimes he would leap from his easy chair with a shout. If my mother was outside hanging up clothes or in the garden, he would rush out to tell her of the event. She was always responsive, showing interest regarding the playoff of the season.

Being of Irish blood, my father was an emotional man. He didn't always keep it covert. Communicating easily with color and no loss of words made him a very interesting and entertaining person. We children enjoyed the funny ditties and tongue twisters he would occasionally tell us. Often they were told when we were helping him pick up potatoes he was digging or some other job we were helping him accomplish. I am sure his motive was in keeping us cheery while we worked.

Along with agriculture, my father became a bee keeper when he was a young man still living with his parents and siblings. He had made the effort to learn all about tame honey bees and how to set up hives for them. He continued beekeeping many years after all we children were born. The honey the bees produced and my father confiscated was a wonderful source of nutrition and a special blessing during hard economic times of the depression era.

Michigan's flora and fauna was of deep interest to my father. Over the years, he gained considerable knowledge of both. By the time I was at the end of my high school years he developed a wildlife habitat on a piece of property of about forty acres with much of it wooded land. My mother had inherited it from her parents. My father spent many weeks hand planting numerous long rows of varied shrubs that were not commonly known in Lower Michigan. I remember one kind was Russian Olive and another Partridgeberry. They were beautiful shrubs that produced red berries in the fall. The purpose of the shrubs was to attract and help sustain wildlife that was gradually diminishing in number. His habitat proved successful in resurrecting ring-necked pheasants, ruffed grouse, quail and likely other birds.

Trees were of great interest to my father. He was able to identify any tree grown in Michigan. He understood the type of lumber each tree produced as well as the grain of the wood. During his lifetime he built two houses from trees he selected from the woods on the farm where we lived. He also built the tiny outhouse and another small building that housed pigs.

Though my father showed much interest in horticulture and agriculture, I think he considered becoming a history professor as his good friend was one and he seemed intrigued with the man. When he graduated from high school his father offered him the opportunity to begin buying a farm of his own at the age of twenty-one. A friend of his father had confided that he would be selling his farm in three years. He inquired if my father chose farming as his life's work if he might be interested in acquiring the farm. I understand my father gave it considerable thought before signing an agreement of purchase at the age of twenty-one.

My father's brother had no desire to make farming his main livelihood. Neither did his father make any mention of financial help of a college education. I believe because of both my father felt obligated to stay with farming and help his father with his farming. He stayed with farming until he was old enough to retire. He and my mother eventually sold their farm and moved to a lake home not far from Traverse City, Michigan. Two of their married children were living in the Acme area about twenty five miles from where my parents decided to retire. My parents lived at their lake home until my father's death in 1983.

My mother grew up mainly on a farm as her father was a farmer. She lived her first twenty-two months in Isabella County near Shepherd, Michigan. Then the family moved to a farm in Oklahoma near Guthrie. She had one brother four years her senior and no sisters. Their upbringing was such that it became no surprise to me that she became a teacher and her brother a farmer and preacher.

After four years, the family needed to leave the area for health reasons. My mother's father was diagnosed with rheumatism. His doctor told him he needed to live in a different climate. He and his wife decided to move back to Michigan where many relatives resided.

My mother was five years old when the family took the train to Michigan. It was a long tiresome ride for them all. After hours of tic-tac-toe and other quiet games the children grew restless and wanted to move around more. Sitting for a long time was very difficult for the children. Mother's brother had a bag of marbles in his pants pocket. They made up a marble game that consisted of trying to keep the marbles in the aisle by rolling them one by one to each other. If one rolled off the aisle the other retrieved it and added it to their collection of marbles already gained. Sometimes the train jarred enough to throw the marbles off course, but the rule held. That was part of the challenge and fun. Not long into the game my mother's father told his wife he disapproved of his innocent little girl bending over and exposing her bloomers. She agreed it was probably time to teach her it was unladylike. He said he would call the children back where the couple was sitting and he would tell the children about the other problems with them playing the game, and she could tell their sweet little girl about being ladylike at another time. His wife smiled in agreement as she sat knitting mittens for the children. After gently motioning the children to him with a pleasant smile, he told them he knew it was hard to sit for a long while and knew they were having fun, but he decided that standing was dangerous and sitting on the aisle would get their nice clothes dirty. He mentioned that someone may need to get into the aisle and that needed to be considered as blocking the aisle just was not a good idea. He told the children he would read stories to them after they put the marbles back in their bag. He explained to them that his legs often ached from sitting and he would get up with them and walk in the aisles once in awhile. The children were disappointed, but quietly and politely gave up their marble game. They knew their daddy expected them to be polite and obedient and they respected him. Many times he had expressed that it may not always feel that Daddy's and Mama's decisions are in their best interest, but they need to know they are. He was a very perceptive and considerate man. Their father motioned for his son to sit beside him and gently patted him on the head. Very carefully, he picked up his beautiful little girl with long black curls, gorgeous blue eyes and peaches and cream complexion. He sat her on his big lap and neatly straightened her dress. The children's mama had a tiny lap as she was a small lady. Their father queried them about their choice of the first story. Both children agreed they would like to hear the story of *Little Red Riding Hood*. Their father agreed, smiled and told them he thought it was a good story.

The children had a good father and mother. Their father was good to their mother and she was very good to him. They all deeply loved each other. Nothing but respect was shown for each other. Their father saw their long ride as a good opportunity to become more involved with his children than was often possible. He realized that it offered his wife some reprieve, too.

My mother was groomed to become a fine and respectable well mannered, considerate true lady. That is exactly how we children came to see her many years later. It was her parent's hope that she would come to know that decent men respect and desire that kind of woman and one day she would marry such a man. Both parents took the responsibility of entertaining their children on the long journey. The children were both well behaved. They enjoyed meals on the train and sleeping in the Pullman car, but were glad when they finally arrived in Michigan.

Many relatives met them. They helped with the many items they had shipped on the train, aside from their luggage they carried with them on the ride. Starting a new life meant many decisions had to be made and lots of work and activity. It was very exciting for the family.

On June 28, 1914 World War I began. My mother's parents moved to Alma and her father went to work for the Republic Truck factory to aid in the war effort by building trucks for the United States Army. Soon after the war ended on November 11, 1918, the family traded their home in the town of Alma as partial payment for a farm not far from Ithaca. My mother and her brother were reared there in a peaceful and quiet home with a humble reverence for God. There was no place for haughtiness in this family.

The Biblical Golden Rule of "Do unto others as you would have them do unto you" was a basic principle to be honored without question. Honesty, high morals, and refined manners became quickly evident to anyone in my mother's presence. Her modest and dignified dress and soft spoken way further exemplified her character of being a respectable lady. Excellent grammar and an exceptional vocabulary were always used in her written or oral communication. Slang was never used and seldom even a colloquialism.

While dating, both parents learned that the other greatly enjoyed reading. My father preferred mainly fiction while my mother enjoyed both fact and fiction. She was amazed at what good authors could conjure up from their imagination and were able to express with flair.

Movies in general disturbed my father as he saw them often lacking reality. After my parents married, they very rarely saw one. I suppose finances had some bearing on it. There certainly was no television for them for many years of their married lives together. They spent almost no money on entertainment over most of their years. My mother's entertainment consisted almost exclusively of church and Sunday school attendance. She did little of that in the first years of caring for her children. It was nearly impossible to do alone. Though my father didn't attend church with her much after their marriage, he did not show resentment that she went. He likely admired and respected her for not compromising her religious beliefs. We children had a good mother who used the positive rather than the negative approach with her children. She would say we were to play in the yard rather than telling us to stay out of the road. She understood that the human nature of children hearing *don'ts* seemed to make young children want to do them. It possibly involved not only her young children. Well, this daughter is not talking.

Being no nagger or mother of idle threats, we knew what she said she meant and she meant what she said. If punishment was in order she punished. We learned to trust her reliable word. If we were ever in a public place and not behaving as our mother deemed we should, she had an easy solution. She just flashed us *the look* which was fast and sure as an arrow in hitting its target. Without a word being spoken it meant *stop* beyond any doubt. It was effective immediately. She was anything but a continual complaining and whiney mother or wife. She was too intelligent for that. We didn't always like boundaries, but neither does a cow that touches an electric fence. We knew there was good reason for the limits she put on us because she had previously told us so. A cow never had that understanding. Our mother was not raising any idiots. We children didn't complain about the food on our plate. We knew that was the meal and there was not going to be another one for several hours. We were hungry and ate it even when it was not the most appealing food. When we were old enough to pick green beans and were taught how not to pull up the plants by the roots in the process, there were times when our mother would ask us to pick them. We might protest mildly on occasion, but our mother was a master at controlling her children with such finesse that we didn't realize it. We would sometimes say it was too hot outside. She didn't argue our point; she agreed it was hot outside. She would just add that it would soon get even hotter and the beans needed to be picked while they were at just the right stage of development and that time was today. She knew very well if we weren't picking beans we would be playing out in the heat. That was deliberately not mentioned. She was too clever for that. She told us the sooner we got done the sooner we could play outside and maybe even in the shade. We picked a large pail of beans in almost no time.

Mother surely had to be a little proud of her success. Her tactic worked almost as well as nursing a hungry baby. I eventually came to realize how amazing my mother was. If she ran out of time to get the green beans prepared for supper because of other work, she would ask us to snip off the ends of the beans later in the day when we tired of playing outside. She knew that is when we would most likely not mind sitting for awhile. We did it without complaint. It is an art, folks. Anyone can master it if they have intention to overcome and are willing to learn the method and apply it.

When we were fortunate enough to go to town for groceries with her, we knew enough not to whine or we would find ourselves sitting in the car while she shopped. My mother never really discussed whining with us. We never heard her do it and knew that patience would pay off. If we were well behaved we knew our mother would tell us each we could pick out maybe two cents worth of treats. Usually they were bubble gum wrapped in a waxy paper and with funnies and a big ball of a sucker. It was so much fun. We were happy and so was our mother.

A grocery wagon came out on rural routes every two weeks if memory serves me well. Sometimes we would need a loaf of bread or other small item. It caused great excitement for us children as it meant a treat was in store for us. On occasion, my mother would ask us to play in the yard near the road and watch for the grocery man. Sometimes he would blow his horn to let us know he was near our driveway. We missed him a few times because we didn't hear him. To us children that was tragic. We lived frugally and spent money very carefully so we were always thrilled if there was something our mother needed because she always saw that a few cents were left over for treats for us. It kept us from forgetting to buy the bread. If there was more change left than needed for our allotted treats, we brought it back to Mama. We often bought BB Bats, which were a small slender wrapped pink taffy candy on a stick for a penny. Bubble gum was always chosen as well. These treats made our day.

Our mother's control in handling her children was commendable. She avoided a lot of chaos and made everyone happier because she cleverly and quite insidiously managed our boundary lines. We knew our boundaries and accepted them knowing they would reliably exist as long as there was a need. Little did we realize that having boundaries gave us security, but they did provide just that. I eventually came to realize how fortunate we were to have such a consistent and wise mother.

After several years of staying home with her children and doing a good job in rearing them, my mother went back to teaching school. My parents really needed the extra income. By the time she went back to teaching school it was mandatory that she take college extension classes to continue teaching. For years she endured the extra burden of the classes offered by the college in Mt. Pleasant, but held in Ithaca. In all, she taught for twenty-seven years. When my mother brought home records for figuring each student's report card grades she kept them private from her children. Since we knew many of the students and other family members she felt we had no business knowing their grades. It was typical of her honorable and admirable morals.

After she retired, my mother looked forward to having time for crosswords and more reading. She taught adult Sunday school classes and enjoyed it. Not long after her retirement, my paternal grandfather was stricken with a serious stroke that left one entire side useless. Grandma had passed away in August of 1950 and his other son and wife had moved in his home and lived with him. It turned out that my parents took Grandpa in after his stoke. My mother was back to caring for a person who needed more care than a baby. My parents gave up their bedroom and put a hospital bed in the room for Grandpa. My father's job was to get him into and out of his wheelchair as it was not something my mother could manage alone. After some years, Grandpa died in their home in April of 1955 at just under eighty-one years old. Four brothers and three sisters preceded him in death. My maternal grandfather passed away in August of that same year.

Grandma was invited to live with my parents. My youngest sister lived there for maybe a year and my brother was there longer. Grandma was pleasant and able to tend to her own needs. She slept in my parent's bedroom as a bathroom was very near. She lived in my parent's home until she passed away in January of 1958. She was a sweet lady with a very pleasant and quick smile. I remember one time she bought a new dress and then afterward was concerned that it may be too gay. (That meant too bold in print or gaudy in her terms.) I remember Grandma was a very modest lady who usually wore navy or dark background print dresses with tiny flowers or some other delicate design. She told us the story of one time when she was much younger she and Grandpa were in Lansing shopping and Grandma was wearing a nice looking hat. They were caught in a sudden rain and her hat began to run with navy blue dye and it was streaking down her face. All she could do was to use her hankie and finally Grandpa's handkerchief to keep wiping the dye away. She said it was probably the most embarrassing event of her life.

After her dear mother passed away, my mother had time to organize her huge button collection. It became such a beautiful and informative collection that the local college asked her to come exhibit and discuss it. She put many hours of research into learning about the old buttons; about what materials were used, where and what years they were made. Some were Goodyear Rubber, some made of carved bone and wood, and a wide array of other products. Some were worn on uniforms during various wars. Others came from high button shoes and many other interesting sources. She also amassed a stamp collection and a large coin collection. All the coins were well sorted and graded for condition. The coins were all placed in coin folders for each of her children at a future date. All her collections were beautifully and neatly done. After my parents moved to their lake home, she continued many months of work on her collections. Living a dull and unproductive life was never my mother's intention.

When my father's health began failing after a few years in their lake home, my mother took care of him. His care became very involved and meant an almost constant vigil on him. Indeed, she did have an active life until shortly before her death. She died just a month short of her ninety-seventh birthday.

My parents about the time of their marriage.

Chapter 2

Dating Daze

Dating in my grandparent's era was usually quite formal. Much of the courtship occurred in the home of the young lady's parents. The men and women usually dressed in their Sunday's best attire. The women often wore stiffly boned corsets under their petticoats and long dresses. Gloves and well adorned hats were customary accessories. They wouldn't be playing tennis, but maybe croquet. A typical date might be an invitation from the lady to her suitor to have dinner and conversation with her parents and other family members who lived in the home. It was a good opportunity for the parents to become acquainted with their daughter's date. The suitor well knew eagle eyes were on him and learning about his character and general mores and observing his behavior toward their daughter.

Marriage is to be a lifetime situation and the parents wanted to be sure it was with a good man. With the suitor being well aware he was being scrutinized, it behooved him to keep his best foot forward. Though he was likely sizing up the family at the same time, they usually had nothing to prove and the challenge was mainly his. If he was seen as a good catch, like coming from a wealthy family, he may find their putting on airs as phony and disgusting. He may see it as them being more interested in what he had than who he is.

In serious relationships, the lady would find herself in her suitor's parent's home. Naturally, she would be on her toes as she was in the same situation of acute observation. Respectable parents placed strict curfews on their daughters in early dating years. The daughters were familiar with their parent's insistence that it was very important for her to protect her name. If curfews and other restrictions were not met, she could be sure of punishment that may be humiliating as well as painful. It would mean a loss of privileges that were meaningful to her. Even if a daughter no longer lived at home, getting home at a respectable hour was firmly stuck in her mind.

Protecting her name was of major importance. She was taught that only decent men were drawn to a decent lady. Not knowing how a prospective mate dealt with life on a normal basis certainly had its risks.

In my grandparent's era, going steady did not mean daily. It usually did not even mean a frequent date or long courtship if there was much travel distance between homes as was often the case in rural courtships. Travel in the winter or spring was often miserable for horses and humans. Snow often made travel difficult or impossible. Spring brought rain and often produced muddy and deeply rutted roads. Finding a mate near one's home was usually uncommon because many relatives often comprised an entire community of several square miles. Selection of a mate was very limited.

Though people were not well acquainted at the time of marriage, divorce was as rare as hen's teeth. It carried a foreboding stigma nobody wanted. A divorcee was marked for life with little to no chance of ever remarrying. In their era more people lived in rural areas than in town. Other factors played a part in no divorce. It was nearly financially impossible without ruining a farmer's livelihood. If children were involved, the situation became even more compromised. Even if a woman was not keen on housekeeping and rearing children, she accepted it as her lot in life if she chose to marry. Husbands chose their careers, but women inherited theirs. It seems that couples simply had lower expectations of marriage in those days. Though some indications were present, a prospective husband couldn't always be sure his wife was a good cook, baker, housekeeper, or would even be a good mother. The wife usually had no assurance that her husband would continue to treat her considerately or that he would earn a reasonable income. Sometimes the income factor was more assuring if she saw that the farm he came from was well managed by the husband's father. The son had usually worked the land with him and understood what his father taught him was involved in successful farming.

In my parent's era, most women worked in the home, particularly if they were farmer's wives. Some had educations that offered a different career which usually was a backup in case it was needed for survival. After World War II began in 1941, it brought lifestyle changes to many homes in America. Though farmers were usually exempt from going to war as they provided food for the nation, many other men did go off to war. Women were needed in factories to take the place of men fighting for their country. Rosie the Riveter became a household name. She exemplified women working in factories. Some women went to war and became a WAC (Women's Army Corps.) member. Others became WAVES (Women Accepted for Voluntary Emergency Service, the women's United States Naval Reserve). Many were educated in nursing and other fields that were applicable.

After the war, many women began working outside the home. They worked as teachers, nurses, beauticians, secretaries, and a variety of other jobs. It often became popular even with children in the home. It resulted in men becoming more involved with their children's care and with some household chores. Life in the home for many became a different environment than in my grandparent's era. In my era, except for farmer's wives when there were many duties like gardening and food preservation, it was common for many women to work outside the home.

In this generation, divorce has become more frequent than in my parent's era. It demanded new coping skills not only for the parents, but their children. Perhaps, in part due to a good economy, the latest generation is different from what their parents experienced. The "living happily ever after" fantasy seems a reality to many when they marry. Young women in particular, are bombarded with movies, television, and magazines that make it seem that marriage is to be a lifetime romance. The truth is that romance is short-lived because it isn't a realistic concept that is compatible with daily life. Couples living together are faced with real problems that demand their attention and solving. Not understanding what marriage really is makes for big problems. The notion that a genuine healthy marriage relationship replaces romance with a deep growing affection and real love has not occurred to them. Their ideas about marriage bring on feelings of being short changed and they become dissatisfied with their spouse. Sometimes they wonder if something is wrong within them or their spouse.

Many young people in America today have only known the good life. Their experience has been having it all with no consideration of the time and effort it took their parents to afford it for them. In some cases, their parents can't afford their lifestyle. They have spoiled their children by spending beyond their means. This sometimes leads to financial disaster for their parents and other serious problems demand they change their ideas of money management. It often leads to disagreements between spouses and sometimes ends in divorce. This adversely affects them, their children and any grandchildren. Sadly, it is a bad situation that could easily be avoided. Their children likely won't even realize what led to the unfortunate outcome. Many newlyweds want it all early in marriage as that is what they have always known. A different concept seems not to be a part of their views. Handling finances leads to disagreements that may not be resolved. Money is often the biggest reason for divorce. Often a relationship ends for that reason. Perhaps divorce today is taken too lightly. The newspaper columns today are nearly as long for divorce as for marriage.

Not much in America is sacred today. Living responsible lives should certainly not be entirely up to the church. Many of the people who need to understand what responsible living entails never step inside a church, so parents need to take the responsibility and teach their children what responsible living is. It needs to be taught starting in their children's formative years.

Maybe if schools made Family Living a required class, some of the young who are not fortunate enough to get instruction in good relationships and responsible living would get the opportunity to acquire that knowledge. The subject matter could contain psychology, parenting, interpersonal relationships, and responsibilities and many related issues. Many young women today think nothing of walking into a bar unaccompanied by a man. They are unaware that they have come to the wrong place for adding true joy to their lives. Many are divorced and are looking for something or someone to fill the void they feel in their lives. Much of the language and behavior of people who frequent these places is crass and disrespectful. Even much of the music played there is of a demonic nature. When live music is offered it is not uncommon to see the musicians behave in a wild manner. The body movements of many dancers are often undignified and nothing like a graceful and beautiful waltz. The attire worn by many young women is disgraceful. Women who wear clothing lacking dignity show they have no self respect. Consequently, they do not attract a gentleman, but only a male who no woman should desire. If a couple of this kind marries, they are not capable of establishing a desirable home. A child born into such an environment becomes a victim and will emulate what he or she learns. This cycle will repeat itself without proper intervention. It becomes a pathetic and difficult chain to break for even the most insightful and best trained individuals to handle with success. It takes a long time to achieve positive results.

Prevention obviously is by far the best way. Somehow people in the dire living circumstances need to be made aware there is a much better way to live. The first thing is to recognize and care that the problem exists. Second, is to believe that proper intervention can change it. Third, is to find people who are willing to get involved. I again stress that it is my belief that with the right people in the school systems from the top down, including the school boards, much can be accomplished where it is not done in the home. I do not expect a sudden change, but believe it needs to begin at young ages. It is possible that the parents need counseling and that may be difficult to arrange and unenforceable. It is a sad and complicated factor of life that needs to be overcome.

Chapter 3

The Car

My father was proud of having a late model car when he began dating my mother. He had a new 1927 Model T Ford that cost around three hundred dollars. Early in their dating my mother told him she was impressed with his car. She complimented him on it being so tidy on the inside and on the outside to the extent that dusty or muddy roads allowed. He told her it was purchased brand new and added that 1927 was the last year the model was built.

Cars were changing American history and my father was aware of some facts regarding them. He mentioned some to his girlfriend. Henry Ford built his first working engine in 1893. He related that the Ford Motor Company incorporated and began building the Model T Ford in 1903. People were very excited about these cars. By 1915, over half a million were produced. Demand became so great that ten million were built by the time the 1924 model emerged. This change from horse and buggy days was brought about by Henry Ford. The horse and buggy era was rapidly phased out in America. Dobbin was being replaced by Tin Lizzies, as they were affectionately called. A horse needed a crack of a whip to start it and hay, oats, and water to keep it going. A Tin Lizzie required the turn of a hand crank to get it started. It needed a radiator filled with water to keep the engine cool and gasoline in a tank for its running energy. Horses needed to be led to a tank for drinking water and they were not always available when the horse needed it. Cars didn't shiver in the cold or swelter on hot days. They had no emotions so they never spooked like a startled horse. Body excrements were left behind a horse. Not only was there a chance of a street pedestrian being splattered by urine, but manure droppings were unsightly and emitted an offensive odor as did expelled methane gas. Flies were attracted to the manure and urine. They disturbed the horses and were a health hazard to humans. Cleaning town and city streets where horses trod was an unpleasant but necessary job. Not many were interested in that sort of work. Cars offered more protection from the elements and were more comfortable and desirable than buggies. It is no wonder that having a car seemed such a luxury.

After nearly a year of my parent's courtship, it advanced from Saturday nights to include Sunday afternoons, then Wednesday nights when possible. An alarming situation occurred one Monday evening that involved my father and would affect my mother. My father's brother paid him a visit with upsetting news for my father. His brother told my father that he had found a lady he interested in wanting to know better. His brother told my father he wanted to use the car on every other Saturday night and every alternate Sunday afternoon; and added that he wanted to use the car this coming Saturday night. He explained that, since he had half ownership in the car, it was only reasonable that it be shared equally. He quickly stated that he had spared my father that for a long time. My father hid his feelings of panic well, smiled and told his brother he appreciated his thoughtfulness. He congratulated his brother upon finding a lady in whom he was interested. He had the presence of mind to remain calm and pleasant as he told his brother that his girlfriend was not aware that he had equal ownership in the car. He hoped that his brother would show some empathy.

His hopes were quickly dashed when his brother told him it was his problem. His brother's voice became a little louder as he told my father he certainly had to be aware that Friday nights did not offer the options of entertainment as did Saturdays. Adding to his complaint, he said his parents went into town right after supper on Friday nights to get groceries and said my father knew their mother didn't drive. He said they often came back with a muddy or dusty car and there was no time for washing it before taking it on a date. My father could see he was becoming more riled as he related the information to him. He quietly listened to his brother as he said his girlfriend would like to hear the Sunday afternoon concerts that were held every two weeks. He said his parents liked to take the car on Sunday afternoon drives and look at crops in the neighborhood and sometimes get an ice cream cone in town. Other Sundays, they sometimes visited relatives. He said when they wanted to go to the concerts that he took them. In a tone of disgust, he said he was not going to ask to use their car anymore. He silently awaited my father's response, not blinking an eye but staring directly at my father. My father forced himself to remain outwardly calm. He told his brother he would see his girlfriend Wednesday night and get back to him regarding her reaction.

That response was not acceptable to his brother. His brother's Irish temper flared, he stepped closer to my father, pointed his finger almost in my father's face and told him in a voice just under a shout that it made no difference to him what his girlfriend's response was as he was demanding the car. My father decided that his calm response to his brother was frustrating him; he acted like he was in the mood for a fist fight. My father was larger than he and told him if he desired to fight to come ahead. His brother stepped back. In still a loud voice he said that all he wanted from him was fair consideration. He gave my father a fierce stare, turned on his heel and walked to his parent's car and gave it a vicious crank and got in the car. It had just occurred to my father that the next Sunday his brother wanted the car was concert day. He stood in a daze at this point. As his brother was ready to drive away he yelled back at my father telling him to count on his using the car Saturday night. My father remained quiet. His brother drove down the road leaving a cloud of dust big enough to choke an elephant.

My father stood for a few moments as he pondered the mess in which he found himself. He had to figure a way to present it in an acceptable manner. He was angry he had missed hearing Gabriel Heater and his news broadcast. Likely, he was more angry with himself for not being up front about the car ownership months ago. My father knew he was in big trouble.

He realized his integrity might be in jeopardy in the eyes of an honorable, innocent lady he greatly admired. He was thinking that half truths were often considered equivalent to prevarication. He thought that may be the view of his girlfriend. Every bit of finesse he could contrive would be necessary on Wednesday night. He feared he may have ruined a relationship with a lady he had grown to greatly enjoy. Before going to see her on Wednesday night, he repeatedly went over the tactics he would use. He had it well rehearsed in his mind. Going to see her was not without trepidation. His feelings three days ago were those of walking on a cloud; now he was trying to walk in quicksand.

After arriving at my mother's parent's home he was determined to appear calm and casual. He kept his outward composure well controlled. He greeted all the family and spent some time in conversation with them. He asked his girlfriend if she would take a short ride with him as he had something to discuss with her. He said he wouldn't keep her up late as they both had to be up early for work the next morning. His girlfriend said it was fine with her. Her parents smiled. She verbally expressed to him privately on their way to the car that she was very anxious to hear what he had to say. That remark sent a sudden chill through my father. It was obvious to his girlfriend that he wasn't as talkative as usual. She considered it was very dark and maybe he was concentrating on seeing the road. My father found a lonely road where they could park for awhile. Neither quite knew what to expect from the other. He asked his girlfriend if parking there met her approval. She told him it would for a short time. It was beginning to rain. She was doubtful anyone would be on the road. No houses being near offered her some comfort. She noticed her boyfriend had not given her a greeting kiss as usual and had a concerned look on his face as he drove. She had become concerned over what he had to tell her. After parking the car, my father had remained behind the steering wheel, but slightly turned in her direction. She stayed near the passenger door and had her body partially turned toward him. Gingerly, my father explained that his brother had stopped by to talk with him. He told her that he had said he would like to more frequently date a lady he was seeing. He wanted to get better acquainted with her by seeing her more. He related that his brother would like to use the car on Saturday nights every other week and Sundays on alternate weeks. He added that his brother explained that Friday nights did not offer the options of entertainment as did Saturday night. She was stunned and began to consider that signs were pointing to the possibility that her boyfriend was wanting out of the relationship. She had come to greatly enjoy it. The thought was very disturbing to her. Suddenly she shifted her body to sitting square on the seat and sat facing the front window. By now both of them seemed to be watching the rain run down on the front window, but with thoughts elsewhere. My father paused, waiting any comment from his girlfriend. She remained quiet, keeping her emotions in check, at least visually. It seemed apparent to my father that she was not acting her normal self. Each had their own concerns and thoughts at the moment. It was time for my father to say he hated to let his brother down and was very disappointed his brother no longer was satisfied with Friday night entertainment. His girlfriend looked his way and said she appreciated his concern for his brother. She then added she admired his compassion in loaning his car to him on Friday nights and his humbleness in not even mentioning it.

My father nearly choked on hearing that. He felt as though he was lung deep in quicksand. Being very aware of his demeanor, my father offered a pleasant smile. Avoiding clarification, he retorted quickly that his brother was planning to soon purchase a new car. She said that would be nice. My father nodded with a smile and remarked that he was happy for his brother and it wouldn't bother him that his brother had a newer car than he. Without hesitation, he further added that he knew how much she liked the car he drove, so it was fine with him. Again my father deliberately paused in hopes she would agree that sharing the car was fine. She remained quiet, but her mind was tossing out thoughts like a whirlwind. The thought crossed my mother's mind that since he was loyal to his brother he would probably be so with a wife. She didn't want to lose him, but indications were still in her mind that it was soon going to be bad news regarding their relationship. She continued to stare at the front window in silence. The deafening silence, except for the pouring rain, lasted too long. It was time for my father to fess up to his girlfriend, come what may.

He mustered up the courage to say he opted to not mention that his brother had equal ownership in the car when they first began dating as he had no idea where dating would go and saw no point in mentioning it. She turned her head sharply toward him. What she just learned was pretty shocking. Almost auctioneer style my father gave no time for verbal response from her. He continued like a gun shot in saying since his brother was planning to buy a car soon, he saw no reason to mention the dual ownership. He was quick with further defense by saying that people buying a house or farm refer to them as their house or farm and a car should be no different.

She sat staring at him. He was very uncomfortable, and it was obvious to her. He shifted his position. She turned her head away from him and again faced the windshield. After a moment of silence, she suddenly gave her neck a sharp turn, looked him square in the face and asked him to get on with what he had to say and get it over. Her reaction came as quite a surprise to my father. He had never seen her anything but calm and patient. It was time for my father to take step number three. He saw no choice now but to risk it would work.

Suddenly, he moved over closer to her and put an arm around her, turned her face toward him and softly said he felt so blessed to have met such a wonderful and beautiful lady. His girlfriend was waiting for the next word to be "but" as he finished his sentence. It felt to her like time was standing still. To my mother's great surprise my father whispered to her that he loved her. He leaned his lips against hers giving her his first ardent kiss. My father decided he needed to distract her thoughts and dull the shock of what she had learned regarding the car and give her something new to toss around in her mind. His timing was perfect; right when my mother was so vulnerable. In an almost quixotic moment my normally cautious and sensible mother that I eventually came to know, responded like butter in the sun telling him she loved him too. My father was cunning as a sly fox. Their courtship continued and so did the sharing of the car.

Chapter 4

The Tiny Abode

Starting married life together in the tiny house was not ideal. Both agreed that being seven months into the throes of the depression, it would be tolerable for maybe three years. My mother said she would try to see it as a camping out adventure, but hopefully they would soon have electricity. The little house was planned to be a workshop as soon as the big one was built. The new house was to be closer to the road and in front of the workshop far enough to be appealing and yet practical. Getting the trees cut and hauled from the woods, and the lumber milled, stacked, and dried took a good year and a half for the little house and privey. In all, it would take about three years to get the larger two-story house erected in any spare time my father could find aside from farming duties. My father told his bride that as soon as the crops were harvested in early fall, he would start cutting the trees, running them through his sawmill, and stacking the lumber to dry. He had built the little one and the small privy two years ago.

While my father lived only part time in the house for the past year, not having electricity was not a big problem. Since he lived mostly at his parent's home, he wasn't in the house enough to warrant electricity. When my father applied for electrical service two weeks before he and my mother were to marry he was shocked by some very bad news. He lived on a road of people of the Mennonite sect who did not believe in using electricity. That meant that until there was greater demand the electric company would not run poles and a line on the road to my parent's house. The depression had affected the electric company like many businesses in America. My father never considered there would be a problem. He didn't know of a mile in all the area that had no electric poles and lines. It was a terrible blow to my parents.

In the fall, my father began cutting the trees and trimming off the branches to make logs. He used two horses pulling a dray to get the logs to his sawmill, which was located just outside the woods. He ran the logs through the sawmill. The logs were turned until a square long bare log was formed. It was run through the mill and sliced into various thicknesses. Then it was cut into different widths and lengths that my father deemed necessary for various parts of building material.

Cutting the wood and handling the logs and lumber was dangerous, difficult, and very arduous work for one person. After the lumber was dry and my father knew which pieces he wanted for wood work and other inside wood like the open stairway, he ran it through a planer he bought when he built the little house. It was a huge heavy piece of machinery that was run by a gasoline engine and a wide belt. The planer smoothed the wood in preparation for fine sanding and varnishing to expose the beautiful grain.

Though crop prices fell by the next year's harvest, my father continued to cut and prepare trees for lumber. He expected, just like last year, to work in snow again until it became too deep. He was anxious to have a workshop and to have his wife living under better conditions.

A baby girl was born in May of 1931, only eleven months after my parents were married. This made the little house seem smaller, despite the thrill of having a new baby. It meant added financial expenses, but my parents managed. My father had planted an orchard on the property before my parents married and it was beginning to produce fruit. A strawberry patch also provided fresh and canned food. My parents had a garden for enjoying fresh vegetables and for canning for the months of no fresh ones. They planted potatoes for long term use and stored them in the basement of my paternal grandparent's house until needed. There were eight crates. Some would be used for seed in the spring.

Like all rooms in the house, the kitchen was very small but the most used. It was not a two adult kitchen. There was little walking space after appliances were in place. On the wall next to my parent's bedroom was an area long enough for a kitchen cook stove with a reservoir. A piece of asbestos was on the wall behind it for fire protection. Next to the cook stove was an opening into my parent's bedroom. The adjacent wall to the dining room had an open doorway and was where the kitchen table and four chairs were. The wall at the opposite end of the stove had a door that led to the washroom. From the corner of that wall and the outside wall that ran almost to my parent's bedroom doorway was a row of storage cabinets and a short counter at one end. There was a sink with little counter space.

With only enough room left between the end of the stove and the end of a narrow base cabinet, was a space just large enough for reasonable access from the kitchen to the bedroom. A small counter beside the sink held a water pail, a dipper for drinking water, and a wash basin. The cabinet underneath contained some wash cloths, hand towels, and kitchen towels on a shelf. Under that shelf were combs, hairbrushes, tooth brushes, and a box of soda for brushing teeth. The bottom shelf held bath towels. A medicine cabinet on the wall above contained my fathers shaving equipment and various medical supplies like tape, gauze, iodine, mercurochrome, aspirin, castor oil, cough syrup, Cloverleaf salve, peroxide, Lysol, Vick's Vapor Rub, and Musterole. (Musterole burned when it was applied to chests when one had a chest cold.)

A large single sink held two dishpans; one for washing and the other for rinsing dishes. It had a drainer tray built in on one end. Underneath was a two-door storage cabinet that held the dishpans, soaps, and cleaning supplies. A drain from the sink ran outside into the nearby orchard area. There was a window above the sink. A metal cabinet, about forty inches long, completed filling the wall length. The top contained a flour bin that held twenty-five pounds of flour. It had a built-in sifter at the bottom. Next was a compartment that held cooking and baking supplies like salt, molasses, honey, corn meal, oatmeal, lard, sugar, coffee, baking powder, yeast, baking soda, cocoa, and spices.

The base portion of the cabinet had an enameled metal counter that stored another pull-out one under it. It provided more depth when making pies or bread or rolling out cookie dough. There was a large area that contained pots and pans with the lids stored in a rack attached to the door. Next to it was a stack of three drawers. The top one held flat wear and one section was for sharp knives and shears. The second drawer held a rolling

pin, pancake turners, potato masher, ricer, shredder, ladles, and other uten-
sils. The bottom drawer was for bread. Dishes, bowls, cups, saucers, drinking glasses, big bowls, and platters were in the step-in pantry just off the
dining area and a few steps from the kitchen. The built in upper cabinets
had glass doors made from window panes and frames. Below the doors was
solid wood painted white. The wall of floor-to-ceiling cabinets also stored
jellies, jams, apple butter, tomatoes, green beans, corn, peas, lima beans,
carrots apple sauce, plums, peaches, strawberries, and many other foods. A
table and six chairs and buffet were on one side of the dining room not far
from a daybed. There was a large framed picture on the wall above the buffet. How well I remember that large sail boat on greenish turbulent water
with ominous clouds above. The dining room and living room combination was heated by a round oak stove. A wall separated the small second
bedroom from the living area. On that wall, directly behind the stove, was
a large piece of asbestos to prevent the wall from becoming too hot. The
stove sat on a large metal mat with asbestos backing to protect the floor.

My mother had a rocking chair and my father a big easy chair that sat
beside a big floor model radio run by a large battery. A well-stocked small
bookcase sat on a wall across from my father's chair. Several of the books
were classic fiction; some were books of poems that included poetry of
Robert Lewis Stevenson, the poem "Abu Ben Adam" by James Henry Leigh
Hunt, and other good oldies. There was a *World Book Encyclopedia* set, a
large *Webster's Dictionary* and the yearly *Almanac*. There were two Bibles
and some of my parent's school books among other non-fiction books. On
top were *The Michigan Farmer*, *The Farm Journal*, and *The Farmer's Wife*
magazines.

My parent's bedroom had a double-size bed and an armoire with a mir-
rored door. Behind it was space to hang a few items that occupied half of
the armoire. The other side contained three drawers with a top for placing
a hand mirror and a comb and brush set. There was a movable mirror on
top at the back of a flat area above the drawers. The room contained two
windows for cross-ventilation and a back combination door with one be-

ing a screen door. My parents felt safe in the neighborhood sleeping on hot summer nights with the solid door open. The only walking space in their bedroom was one aisle at the end of their bed and one side of the bed. The other side was nearly against the wall opposite the walkway. A small walk-in closet had a few deep shelves and a board on the wall that held hooks was just off the bedroom.

A small porch was at the front of the house. The upper half was screened with wood below on the bottom. A rubber runner floor mat helped catch the dirt from feet before it was tracked inside the house. The entry doors to the porch and living area of the house were directly in line with each other so the full length runner worked well. The light grey painted cement floor provided a surface that was easily mopped and one that rain wouldn't destroy. There was no porch furniture. When company dropped in on a warm day the dining room table chairs were taken out to provide a place to sit.

All the floors inside the house were covered with linoleum. The washroom floor was the same as the porch surface. The rustic room was just off the kitchen. It held a gasoline engine-run, crank ringer washing machine, and other items. Later a cream separator was used to make and sell cream instead of whole milk. The defatted milk was fed to the pigs. A long narrow stand held two tubs next to the washing machine for a first and second clothes rinse. An ample rectangular three foot high built-in hamper was in one corner of the room next to the kitchen door. It was the only hamper in the tiny abode. Two galvanized pails sat on the floor for carrying water. A five-gallon slop bucket that held potato peels, apple cores and peelings, whey, and other items the pigs ate was on the floor in the rustic room. A copper boiler sat on a shelf and was used to heat water on laundry days, for canning, and heating bathwater. A covered enameled diaper pail and potty chair were soon added. Mama had a lid covered pail for soaking rags she used for later washing.

Shelves were built on the two outside walls for storing empty canning jars, lids, a large canning pot and lid, crocks, and other such needed items. Homemade soap that was made from lard and lye and a few bars of Fel's Naptha soap that worked well on my father's greasy and badly soiled work clothes were among other shelf items. The house was a very compact place to live. The kitchen was often uncomfortably warm for my mother. It was where she spent many hours of her day and where she softly sang hymns and wiped off perspiration while she worked. For many years, water was hand-pumped from a well near the house. A planked walkway led from the laundry room to the pump about twenty-five feet away. Another planked walkway led to the privy that is also called an outhouse. It was a necessary little place that was miserably cold in the winter and smelly in the summer. On its seat with two holes was ample space for outdated catalogs that were used for purposes other than the original intent. Its occupants usually made a fast exit. It is understandable that my mother thought of living in the surroundings as camping out. If she had known how long she were going to be living where she agreed to in the beginning it would seem she would have considered it impossible to tolerate.

Chapter 5

A New Baby

On a sunny July day in 1932 my parents had been married two years and a month, the wheat crop was ready for harvest and the weather was perfect. Harvest wouldn't happen today as indications were that they would be adding a new family member. Their little girl was fourteen months old. Like all farmers, my father was hoping for a boy. After several hours of misery my mother gave birth in the little house. I was that baby, but instead of being named Phillip, I was given the name of Phyllis. Daddy would love me anyway. My sister couldn't say my name well and called me Fiss. I didn't mind that I wore hand-me-down clothes like navel bands, undershirts, and kimonos with two front sets of ties, rubber pants, booties, and other items. Diapers were made from white flannel squares. I may have had some smaller ones Mama made for Oleta when she was little. She probably made me a new blanket so my sister could keep hers.

In the beginning all I wanted was my comfort and I wanted it when I wanted it. That innate innocent selfish stage has to be for the purpose of survival. Eventually, it needs to be overcome to make life better for those in the presence of the child and finally for joy for the child directly involved. At first I didn't know much except to cry when I wanted something. I did recognize my mothers voice because I had heard it before I was born. I slept in the little bassinet my sister used when she was tiny. Daddy and Mama bought her a crib a few months after she was born. My sister, Oleta, became a heavy baby and wasn't walking when I was born so Mama sometimes had to carry two babies. Oleta's name came from Mama's middle name which was the name of an American Indian lady my maternal grandma befriended.

Mama often put my sister in a jumper that hung from the kitchen ceiling near the washroom wall. Jumping strengthened her chubby legs and she was where Mama and she could see each other. Oleta had a new wooden highchair that sat in the corner near the kitchen table. The kitchen was really crowded with two added items after the children were born.

Many years later I came to realize and appreciate the labor and other miseries my mama endured during her pregnancies, deliveries, and birthing aftermath. There were plenty more. Her babies were born with no doctor until moments before the baby was delivered. It had to be a frightening experience. Her doctor had patients in his office who needed his attention so he couldn't sit around watching a woman in labor. He had about a four mile drive out to our little house.

Many years would pass before I realized how hard Mama worked and the many sacrifices she made in caring for her children. Today it seems incredible that Mama accomplished all she did under less than ideal circumstances. Farmer's wives did plenty besides caring for their children. They fixed three meals a day for their hungry husbands and much of the two meals came from the garden. Even under ideal conditions, caring for two babies and doing their other duties was about all a mother and wife could handle. Women were told to stay in bed much longer after giving birth than they are today. I am sure Mama could not do it for all of her deliveries.

New mothers never get enough sleep so they are always tired. But with two babies, nothing can be put on hold. Mama endured interruptions of other work all day long and while sleeping as newborns are usually fed every four hours round the clock. That involves diaper changes and burping their babies before putting them back to bed.

Daddy pumped, carried water and filled the copper boiler for heating on laundry days for a while after Mama gave birth. He had to carry the heated water into the washroom and pour it into the washer. Daddy dumped the water after the laundry was done as it had to be carried out in buckets and thrown into the orchard. At least the kitchen sink had a pipe that allowed the water to run into the orchard.

Doing laundry was a big job. Using the hand crank ringer took time. So did hanging clothes on the line, then taking them down for folding or ironing. Fabrics in my mother's era were hard to iron. They often required starch to look good. It was often made at home, put in a sprinkler bottle and applied to the garments. The iron had a removable handle and two flat iron pieces that were heated on top of the cook stove. The iron pieces were exchanged as the iron being used became too cool. The handle was removed from one and attached to the other. It was easy to scorch things as there was no way to regulate the temperature. Having no sanitary napkins added more unpleasant work. Rags that were used were soaked in a covered pail of water, then when full were rinsed in fresh water and finally hand washed. Using an outside privy was a very unpleasant experience, particularly in cold weather.

Most people in America today take modern conveniences for granted. Giving thought to how people in the past have lived should bring great appreciation for what is now available. Camping out is fun for awhile, but not for long. My mother lived in this type of situation for many years. Being the firstborn and getting much attention from parents as well as relatives lessened after another baby entered the family. It was unpleasant at times for my older sister who was born only fourteen months earlier. She was likely weaned from breast feeding at a young age. Of course we each have no control over our order of birth; it is just our lot in life. Perhaps any negative ideas are challenges that need to be overcome.

Children often find it difficult to share their toys. A normal response is "mine." The concept of sharing needs to be taught, learned, and overcome. This applies in dealing with negative ideas that may result from one's birth order. If they are of an unconscious nature, they cannot be resolved until they are brought to the attention of the one harboring the negative, often warped ideas. Overcoming these ideas requires conscious effort. Some children throw a screaming and crying tantrum in public places with no consideration of how strangers view them. They feel no embarrassment. That indicates that self awareness develops over time. Children need much rearing and mother is usually the coach. It is common for a mother to observe spats among her children. She usually does not have to be a referee because they soon end with the children playing together like nothing negative happened. This makes it difficult for even the most astute mother to detect subtle signs of underlying hostility that may only become overt many years later when the individual no longer lives in the home. That is why it often is not recognized during the very important formative years when it needs to be handled. The imagined thoughts of other family members are not realistic since the person to whom they are directed may not have an idea that the other harbors them.

This often produces a sad outcome for both as each becomes a victim of circumstances until the conflict is brought out and resolved. It is common for the beholder to hold a love-hate feeling toward the other person. It behooves a parent to explain to the firstborn that the second child has the same right to have the same good care, attention, and love as the firstborn had.

Adding that mothers love all their children is reassuring. It may be the key to helping the young child overcome negative ideas. A few minutes of explaining, that the mother knows that having to share toys and attention is not always what the child wants at the moment, is a good tactic. The child is reassured by the mother's understanding. She tells the child that people need to share in life just like Mama shares her time with her children. She further explains that sharing makes life happier for everyone. It may be a good preventive intervention to prevent further problems. Such teaching often needs to be repeated several times. If children are taught to treat others like they desire to be treated early they are able to grasp the concept at a fairly young age. Their understanding is often beyond what parents expect. I have seen mothers carefully bite a child back after being bitten by one. It teaches them very quickly not to bite people. The baby who is usually cutting teeth produces a very startled look that tells all. Some believe it is sending a mixed message to the child as the mother just did what a child is not supposed to do, but if she says," No. "at the same moment, the child understands why the mother bit. If it happens again, and the same treatment is used, it is likely the child will have learned not to do it anymore because the mother only bites when the baby bites her. It is akin to fighting fire with fire.

Child rearing requires continual hard work and sacrifice from the mother. It is a complex job that even the most astute mothers find challenging. It becomes more challenging as more children are born. There are more personalities to deal with in less time for the mother. It requires continual attention and the intention of the parents to see that the child learns and overcomes what is innate nature. I think of it as being fine tuned, like God wants His children to become.

Oleta and Phyllis out in the early sun enjoying their very own chairs.
(the author on left)

Chapter 6

February 1934

The post-depression era wreaked havoc all over America. Crop prices plummeted for too long. Many people had not recovered from lost homes. It began to make my parents happy they had the one they did, even if there was no running water, bathroom, or electricity and it had grown crowded.

Daddy felt he needed to have a son born soon as he was thirty-four years old. He would be fifty-two in eighteen years after their third child was born. My parents were so hoping for a baby boy, but instead of being named Charles like her grandfather, she was named Charlene. Daddy and Mama were very disappointed they didn't have a son. Oleta was two years and nine months old and I was nineteen months old when baby Charlene was born. Now they had three little girls who were all babies. Mama had just gotten one child potty trained and now she had two in diapers. Potty training me meant keeping an eye on the clock as Mama attempted to sit me on the pot at the right times.

Charlene was born in winter so Daddy was more help to Mama than when I was born. My birth was at a very busy time for my Daddy. He did some of the cooking and dishes for a few days following Charlene's birth and helped care for the other children as Mama needed help. Throughout the winter he helped with some of the cooking and other things like keeping snow removed from the boardwalks and the driveway. There was only room for one cook at a time, but Mama had plenty of other things to do while Daddy cooked. He did all the grocery shopping; mainly coffee, tea, oatmeal, barley, flour, yeast, sugar, oatmeal, tea, and soaps. The soaps were Ivory Flakes Mama used for their children's diapers and other clothing and dishes. Ivory bar soap was used for bathing her little ones. Mama always kept a bar of Fel's Naptha soap handy for Daddy's work clothes and his greasy hands.

Daddy gathered and heated water for laundry days and took care of clean-up afterward. Carrying out laundry water was heavy work. We children were bathed in one of the tubs once or twice a week. Sometimes we sat on the sink drainer or down in the sink.

Mama ordered needed items from catalogs such as *Sears Roebuck* and *Montgomery Wards*. Only bare necessities were purchased. Sometimes she ordered remnants of material to make her little girl's dresses. Oleta usually got them as she had outgrown hers, but I could wear them.

Daddy did not cut any more trees last fall and early winter as it became apparent the house building would have to be delayed because of daily living expenses and less money coming in. He did sell some cow's milk beyond what we used, but the price greatly dropped over time. He made Oleta a twin bed that was in the second bedroom. I used the crib until Charlene outgrew the bassinet that Oleta and I had used. By June, I was sleeping in the twin bed with Oleta. It had a rail on the open side to keep us from falling off the bed. The crib that Charlene, who was four months old, now slept in was on the other side of the tiny room.

Mama had a very busy summer with her three little girls and all her other duties. She still had a baby to nurse during the night, but only one in diapers. More gardening and canning needed to be done each year. She never had time to stretch out awhile on the daybed when her little ones slept, as that was when she could get in the garden and pick berries and other foods and prepare them for what she intended. She spent almost all her time home with the children. She must have gotten tired of it.

Daddy wouldn't go to church with her and there was no way she could go to the small local country church with three little girls who were babies. After being ousted from his church membership for hunting rabbits on Sunday afternoons, Daddy lost faith in organized religion. He never saw it as a Biblical principle and felt he was wrongly accused of sin that was unjustified. He maintained that his attending church simply made him a hypocrite.

There was no baby buggy. With two little children at her sides and one in her arms, picking up groceries and getting the babies back in the car was a big, time consuming struggle. It had to be done before the children's naps and not at breast feeding time, so Daddy did the job when he could. If Daddy needed a part for a piece of machinery, he would make a quick dash into the grocery store and pick up something Mama needed. He tried using a rainy day for the bulk of the grocery shopping. Other times, he took the time to do it.

In later years of my life, Mama told me I was a busier little one than my sister Oleta. I think she was really saying I was more difficult to watch as I didn't stay in one place very long. Oleta was content with her little books while I played with toys like my top and things that moved like a big ball. Mama also told me when I couldn't have or do something that I wanted I would bang my head on the floor. If I didn't stop when she said to I got my rounded posterior warmed with her hand. Mama taught me to learn to accept options as she guessed I was just bored. It wasn't unusual for me to pout with firmly crossed arms. Mama tried to distract me from it. Sometimes she would ask me to bring her a diaper or something else. She knew I liked being busy and it saved her a few steps, so had dual purpose. She was good about taking the time to explain why she had to tell me no. Sometimes she would move my little rocker where I could see her working in the kitchen and tell me to get my doll and rock her. She said I would hold my big rag doll and rock her for quite awhile. Sometimes Oleta and I both rocked our big rag dolls named Susie and Dutchy.

Mama was a wise, kind and patient mother. She realized my limited vocabulary kept me from the oral expression I desired. She taught me to tell her I was upset rather than throw a conniption fit and she wouldn't need to spank me. She said she didn't like to do it, but when I misbehaved it had to be done. Mama added that when I wasn't crying I could hear her and she could hear me, and together we could find something else to do that maybe I hadn't thought about. Her controlled patience and effort was not in vain as the problem was soon overcome. When I was still a baby in a highchair Mama noticed I might be left handed. She deliberately handed things to me near my right hand for a test. I would take them in that hand and immediately transfer them to my left. She told me later that trying to

41

change a person from left to right handed was thought to sometimes cause stuttering and she did not want a teacher to try to make me do things with my right hand that I wouldn't do naturally. She was an alert mother despite all her cares.

I remain very grateful to her for her being alert to that. As it is, I am an artist of sorts and greatly enjoy painting portraits, landscapes and still life. Long after I was married and with six children, I decided to attend an adult education art class at the local high school for a few weeks. The instructor told me she could be of no help to me as she couldn't paint as well as I did. I did well and had three published in a local paper. When I was in high school, I asked if art might be offered in our school but had no success. I felt it was an area where I had talent.

Since I started nursing school after high school, then married and had a large family, there was little time to become involved in art work. Two of my art works are hanging on the walls of our home office and I gave one to a friend who lives far away and whom I have not seen in years. Today, I do oil and acrylic paintings and have done two large murals. I am left handed as are about 7 percent of the population. I wonder if my God-given talent would have been lost had a teacher insisted that I use my right hand. In my case, it would have not been the right, but wrong hand.

Chapter 7

The Fight

When I was close to three years old an incident occurred one night that changed how I felt about the dark. Until then I had no fear of it. One extremely cold winter night Daddy's hunting dog followed him into the washroom after he came from the barn with my father who had been there milking cows. Daddy let him inside the room for the night. A barn cat had also followed probably smelling the warm milk. Daddy had already closed the barn door and the cat slipped in with the dog. Not wanting to go back to the barn and try to lure the cat in, Daddy allowed it stay in the warm area.

Other than one kerosene lamp burning in the dining room, the only light came from the heating stove. The fire in the stove gave some glimmering light from the isinglass (mica) windows of the stove door. The kitchen only had light that came from the doorway between the kitchen and dining room. The door to the washroom wasn't easily visible.

I needed to use the potty and the little chair was still in the cold washroom. It was set inside the kitchen overnight but that hadn't been done yet. The moment I opened the door and took my first step into the washroom a fight broke out between the cat and dog. The cat flew just over my head after the dog. It was apparent the cat was on the clothes hamper and the dog must have wanted to be there as well. It was built right next to the warm kitchen wall. There would have been room enough for both animals to curl up, but the cat must have thought the dog was stalking it. The cat let out a terrible screeching-like howl the moment it attacked the dog. It was very loud and right beside me. The dog gave a fierce snarl and snapped at the cat. A nasty fight began and the cat jumped back on the hamper in self-defense. The fight stopped immediately, but before it ended I was gone like a dart. I turned and rushed into the kitchen with fear like I had never experienced. I slammed the door in an instant and ran into the dining room to tell Mama. I couldn't speak a word. Being totally speechless was a helpless feeling. I was trembling all over.

Mama said she had heard the fight and by the time she could get up to come to me, I was at her side. She pulled off my wet underwear and picked me up and held me telling me the animals weren't after me and explained what was going on between them. She didn't take time to wipe up the water trail I left, that could wait. Consoling me was of prime importance. After I calmed down, Mama carried me to the kitchen and washed me off. Then she took me to my bedroom and helped me put on my pajamas. She told me she would put the potty chair in the kitchen a little later. First she said she would read me and the others a story. She sat on the end of the twin bed, where Oleta and I were, and read us a happy story that hopefully would make me feel calmer. When the story was done I was not feeling sleepy, but it helped to calm me as did the explaining about the fight.

Mama taught us the prayer of, "Now I lay me down to sleep, I pray the Lord my soul to keep. If I should die before I wake, I pray the Lord my soul to take."

In retrospect, I am a bit surprised that was one she chose. It was one she always said as a young girl with no apparent fear of falling asleep and deemed it all right for us. After we said our prayers, we all shared a good night kiss with Mama.

The last thing I said to her was, "Leave a light on tonight."

Mama said she would. It became a nightly routine that lasted for many years. She never failed to leave a light at night. She just turned the lamp down on dim. As I write this story, I wonder how much extra kerosene we burned over the years. I am sure my parents would have gone without eating, if necessary, to have enough kerosene to keep the lamp burning. Both felt very sorry about my very traumatic experience and Mama said she would always bring the potty chair inside just before blowing out the kitchen light. She did it faithfully from then on for some years.

My parents never tried to rush me in getting over wanting a light left on at night. We had two kinds of lamps, but usually only used one at a time. One had twin mantles inside a globe. The mantles were a mesh-like material made from a cerium compound of a grey chemical element of the rare-earth group. They would turn white while they were burning and produced a brighter white light than the other kerosene lamp. It had a wide tightly woven flat cotton cord that was the wick which absorbed kerosene. Most of it was curled up in the clear glass lamp base, then threaded up through a slit that held it in place. When that upper part was lighted by a match the kerosene caused the wick to burn slowly. The higher the wick was turned up, the faster it burned. The light became brighter which was the purpose in exposing more of the wick above the slit. A clear glass chimney was placed over it to keep drafts off and make it burn with less smoke. It provided protection from an open flame, but the chimney became hot enough to burn you if you touched it. With no electricity, we just accepted our situation. I never recall ever hearing anyone complain about the house being too dark. When Mama sewed on her Ruby sewing machine in the evening after her children were in bed, I am sure the lighting was less than adequate, but she just did what she needed to and did it with grace. Sometimes, she would make something new and other times she sewed a patch on Daddy's work clothes. She put in incredibly long and hard days of work.

Chapter 8

1935

Mama picked strawberries, peas, green beans, carrots, red beets, radishes, onions, cucumbers, tomatoes, various greens, and sweet corn when they were ready to eat and can. Daddy picked plums, peaches, apricots, apples, and some grapes. Poor Mama canned all sorts of foods until days before another baby arrived. She had to have been exhausted by the end of each day. All her duties had to be met on demand as none could be delayed. That included caring for her three children and fixing three meals a day.

There were almost insurmountable tasks to accomplish daily. Having been reared in a quiet and adequate home with no younger siblings and only one older brother, it would seem the circumstances of her life would have been daunting. She dealt with or overcame each situation like a brave soldier. Daddy worked like a trooper, too. He had extra burdens in late summer and fall that came at a very busy time of the year. Mama needed some help with water carrying and picking fruit and other things. August, September, and October were big canning months. Being seven, eight, and nine months pregnant made picking garden foods especially hard. Daddy helped when he could.

In late October of 1935, Mama and Daddy had their first glimpse of their fourth baby. Patrick James was not to be the baby's name; she was named Patricia Jane. It seemed it was an uncontrolled instant reaction that Mama cried and tears ran down Daddy's face as they found they still had no son. Only after I was married and with children of my own did I learn how disappointed they were; but, she was quick to add that after a few minutes they found they loved their sweet little daughter and were grateful she was a healthy baby. She said they never planned for another child after the birth of their fourth daughter.

My parents thought it a possibility their parents might think them foolish to be having so many children so close together in such tough times.

When Patricia was born Oleta was four years and five months old, I was three years and three months and Charlene one year and eight months old.

Daddy had finished harvesting crops. The barn mow had plenty of hay. The oat bin in the granary was as full as Daddy wanted it and so was the corn crib. The purpose of the stored crops and hay was to feed the chickens, horses, pigs, and cows. The other crops were sold to make the farm payment and provide money for daily living. Pumpkins and Hubbard squash were placed in the cool oats in the bin for short-term storage. The watermelons, that had been there, were already eaten, the pigs got the rinds. There was always a slop bucket in the washroom that held apple and potato peelings and other things that pigs would eat. The bees provided enough honey that there was some left to sell after saving some for the family. Daddy dug all the potatoes that were left in the ground. He picked the late apples and crated what wasn't needed immediately and took them to the cellar of his parent's house for cool storage and made cider of some of the apples.

Daddy helped Mama with meals and dishes while she was recuperating from giving birth. He helped with water for laundry and other things like gathering eggs and cleaning and crating them for selling throughout the winter. He had animals and chickens to feed and water and machinery to work on for the next season. He milked the cows in the morning and evening every day and bought groceries. Ten days after Patricia was born, Daddy and Grandpa butchered a hog and shared the meat. Daddy made our share into bacon, side pork, spare ribs, chops, ham, and summer sausage. After they were smoked and treated with Morton's preserving salt, he stored them in muslin casing he made on the sewing machine and the meats were hung from the washroom rafters on hooks for more curing. It was so good and such a wonderful help in providing food for the family for several months. We were fortunate that we could nearly live off the land.

We children had never tasted soda pop. After a few days the cider began to develop a bite and bit of fizz. Our parents had fun watching us take the first sip from a glass as we grimaced in surprise. Once we knew what to expect we began to rather like the taste. That didn't last long because it began turning into vinegar. Eventually, a stringy and slimy brownish substance formed in it. Mama told us it is called "mother," Although I don't recall she told us why. As long as the vinegar lasted, Mama, occasionally strained the mother from it and got rid of the awful looking stuff.

With Mama having birthed four children between 1931 and 1935, our tiny house seemed to be growing smaller as the children grew larger. As soon as Patricia was too big for the well used bassinet, she began using the crib. Daddy had made another bed that matched the twin bed Oleta and I slept in. He stacked the beds into bunk beds. Charlene began sleeping in the bed close to the floor and Oleta and I slept on the top one. I liked climbing up the ladder. Patricia's crib was next to the wall across from the bunk beds.

We three children began calling Patricia, Honey. That came about as Mama asked if someone would see what little Honey wanted when she was fussing in her crib.

Being the busy one, I ran to her and asked, "Whatcha want, Honey?"

I told Mama Honey wanted her diapers changed and to get out of the crib. Mama asked me to play Peek-a-Boo with her and she would be there in a minute. I asked Mama if I could rock her and Mama said I could sit in her rocking chair and rock her after she brought me a pillow for her head. I loved rocking Honey. I talked to her a little bit and she smiled. Pretty soon she began to suck her thumb. I thought it was cute. She stared up at me, but her eyes began closing more and more. Soon she was asleep and Mama put her back in her crib. None of the other children sucked their thumb, but Charlene occasionally sucked her toe. She did this a short while when she was maybe six to nine months old. Charlene was a wiry little thing. She was walking well when Patricia was born, but couldn't always keep up with her two older sisters. She liked sticking near her mama. Sometimes Mama would put her in the highchair and give her a Christmas catalog. She liked looking at the dolls and other toys. It entertained her for about a half hour. Mama didn't want little children running around in the kitchen as there was little room for her to walk. She also felt it wasn't a safe place for a little child.

My parents found it interesting to note we all looked quite different and had different personalities. I favored Daddy some in facial features and Charlene greatly favored Mama. She was a beautiful little girl with black curly hair and blue eyes.

In the winter after Patricia was a few months old, Mama started going back to church. She was a very modest lady and didn't like being in public when she was looking pregnant. It was called "being in a bad way." Mama didn't like that. She was too dignified to be seen in that light and it was a term she never used. Her other children were getting old enough to sit through church. Sunday school and church was a little long for me and Charlene and no nursery was provided, so sometimes she would go just for Sunday school and miss the church service.

Mama knew the spring and summer would mean a lot of hard work, but she was glad to have us all outside breathing fresh air. Being cooped up in a crowded house, where we breathed smoke when the stove doors were opened to add wood was not the best situation. People in that era didn't know asbestos was bad for the lungs and probably didn't give the smoke much thought. It was a necessary evil that came with heat. We had lots of wood that needed to be burned. Daddy got it out of the woods for heat in the Round Oak stove. He stacked it in a huge pile and periodically brought some in the washroom to dry. He kept a little coal on hand to keep the fire burning on the coldest winter nights.

I am sure when spring came Mama was glad to have her rambunctious children outside using up energy in wide open space, as well as giving some consideration to fresh air for our lungs. She got the wagon from the barn that we got for Christmas over a year ago. She washed it off and it was bright red and shiny like it was when we last played with it. It was our only outdoor toy and we played with it much of the time. Sometimes we collected dandelions for a bouquet for Mama. She always thanked us and put them in a vase, and then they closed up and drooped as it became dark. She was very thoughtful. Other times we gathered the burrs from burdock plants and made little baskets out of them. They stuck together so well we children couldn't get them apart. The handles stayed on well. The inventor of Velcro got his idea by examining the burrs up close and copying them.

One day in the summer Charlene and I went to the barn to play in the mow. We climbed the ladder that ended where a two-by-six connected another ladder across the other mow from where we were playing. I spotted a bird's nest on the board and began crawling out on it to see if it had eggs or baby birds in it. Charlene had come down off the ladder and was waiting in the hay beside the ladder. Between the mows was an area where Daddy stored machinery in the off seasons of their use. The distance from the ground to the board I was on was at least twenty feet. A fall that distance or even landing on the machinery would be disastrous. Mama came out to check on us and was horrified to find me sitting as I straddled the board scooting myself along to get to the bird's nest. She deliberately avoided Charlene's or my view of her. She stood frozen in fright as she quietly watched me. She knew any distraction could mean I could fall. I am sure she was praying like never before. She saw me look in the nest and heard me tell Charlene that it had eggs in it. I knew mama bird would soon be back and I needed to get myself down. I knew she may attack me. While in a sitting position, I slowly scooted myself backward on the board, far enough that when lying down, I could bend my legs at the hips so they needed to extend far beyond the board. That was on the hay mow side. Then I needed to turn my body to get my legs on the ladder. That was the hard part. I managed to do it and get back to the hay.

Mama called us down from the mow. She told us to take the short ladder near the horses, so we did. When we got down Mama was shaking and looking very pale. In naive innocence I asked her what was wrong. In a trembling voice she told us when she saw me on the board she was shaken with fright and why she still was shaking. Without hesitation Mama made it very clear that I nor any of the children were never to crawl on that board again. I told her I would never do it again and didn't. Charlene vowed she would never do it and never did. I am not saying we never did any dangerous things after that; they were just of a different kind. I wonder what sort of people we would have become if we never had fun for all the years we struggled through the depression. I doubt anyone would want to be in our company today.

Chapter 9

Phyllis is Missing

One nice day of Indian summer, Mama was hanging out the laundry and I was bored. I told her I missed my sister and wanted to go to school and see her. Mama told me I could go when the school put on their Christmas program. I said that wouldn't be for a long time. Mama ignored that and said I could sit right with her in the seat at her desk. She said there would be a huge Christmas tree decorated with many colors of lights and tinsel and ornaments and would be beautiful. The smell of the pine tree would make the school room smell nice. She told me there would be presents on and under the tree and one for me. I went to find Charlene and told her. I said when she went to visit that she would probably get one, too. It excited us both. We played with the wagon awhile. Honey sat on an Indian blanket on the grass near the clothes lines and watched us. After a while she was fussing a little and Charlene went to play with her.

I was soon back pestering Mama about wanting to go to school. Mama tried to distract me again. She said Halloween was coming in only a few weeks and she would carve a big pumpkin into a Jack O' Lantern. She said we could watch. Mama went on to explain that first she would cut it and make the top like a lid so she could reach in and clean out all the big seeds and stringy parts inside it. Then she would carve a funny face on the front of the pumpkin, then she would put a candle inside the hollowed out pumpkin and light it. When it sat in a dark place the light from the candle would show a funny face. Mama said she would put the Jack O' Lantern on top of the barrel of pickles on the porch and face it where we could see its face through the front window while we were inside where it was warm. She said after Halloween was over she would make pumpkin pies out of it. Charlene heard what she said and we both thought it would be fun to see. I sat on the blanket beside Charlene and we talked about it awhile and I tickled Honey on the toes and made her giggle.

52

I came back again and asked if I could go to school. Mama said she told me "No!" She again tried distracting me by telling me in about only a month after Halloween would be Thanksgiving Day and we would be going to Grandpa and Grandma's house to see them and some cousins. She said we would have a big, delicious turkey dinner and have fun with the others there. Mama said we would draw names for Christmas that would be only about a month away. I told Mama all these things would be fun but, I still wanted to go to school. I told her I couldn't wait to see what school was like. Mama explained that it meant sitting in a seat at a desk with a top that lifted up so the students could reach their school things inside the desk. Each person had to stay in their seat until the teacher called them up for class. They were not to talk aloud until the teacher said they should. Mama told me I wasn't ready to sit at a desk and not talk for a long time, but next school year I would be ready. I told Mama I wouldn't be there very long because Oleta had been gone a long time. I told her I would be quiet and sit quietly in the seat with my sister. Mama had become tired of her tactics that weren't working and my protest had continued too long.

So she said, "Well, go on then."

I took her seriously and left for school. Maybe it was a bad time of month for her because it was totally unlike her to say something she didn't mean. She had been patient and kind in trying to give me some pleasant things to ponder, but finally was just fed up with my persistence. She had the clothes hung up and took Patricia inside and Charlene followed. She put Patricia in the jumper and Charlene in the highchair and gave her a catalog. In a few minutes Mama went out to pull sheets off the line. After she got them down she took them inside and put them on the beds she would make. She returned to the washroom and ran another rinse load of clothes into the basket and took it outside to hang up the items. It occurred to her she hadn't seen me for a few minutes. She looked around and didn't see me. She called for me and I didn't answer. She looked in the house and again back outside. I was nowhere in sight. Mama walked to the barn and stepped inside and called my name and there was no response. She looked in the car and rushed up the driveway looking down the road. She saw no sign of me. She looked in the near fruit trees in case I had climbed one. Again she called and had no response. She felt very doubtful I even knew how to get to the school. She never thought I would take her seriously, but it was beginning to look like I had. She was now frantic.

I was barefoot and my dress probably wasn't clean nor was my hair combed as she started laundry early. She felt I probably had dirty hands and wasn't sure about my face. She pulled Charlene out of the highchair and told her she couldn't find me and needed to get in the car and go looking. She grabbed her purse and carried Patricia and Charlene followed her. In a flash she had her little ones in the car and was headed down the graveled road towards school .Her eyes were scanning the neighbor's homes and watching all around the area as she slowly drove. Her heart was pounding. She saw no sign of me; watching the field on the left side of the road in case I had cut cross lots. She turned the corner to the left after looking both directions carefully. It wasn't traffic that concerned her. There was little traffic on either road she was traveling and I was no where in sight clear to the hill a half mile away. Just as she crested the hill she spotted me running. I wasn't far from our church where she knew I could see the school house a short distance ahead.

Mama pulled the car up near me, stopped and told me to get in. She said she had something to tell me and drove into the church parking area.

I said, "Mama, the school is down there," as I pointed.

Mama said she knew, but we weren't going there. Tears welled up in her eyes and mine. I was shocked she that wasn't taking me there. Mama realized I was upset and considered that she may have made the worst mistake of her life. Mama reached toward the back seat for my hand that was clinging to the back of Patricia's seat. She tearfully and sadly told me she was very sorry she said something she really didn't mean because she didn't think I knew the way to school and wouldn't try to go. She explained that people don't go to school barefooted and without looking neat and clean and that's why she bought and made all the things she did for Oleta. She told me she was not scolding me, because she was in the wrong and not me. She said I didn't have a lunchbox and Oleta only had enough food for herself. I cried, then wiped my tears with my hand and left dirty streaks across my face. Mama showed me in the mirror that I couldn't go to school looking like that. She said she had another idea that she thought I would like. Mama said we weren't far from the Newark Store and she would drive there and buy us all an ice cream cone, because she thought I would be hungry and warm from my long walk. Also, she said she made a bad mistake she would never do again and she was just very sorry and wanted to do something nice for me for disappointing me so badly. Mama squeezed my hand a little. She was looking directly at me as she asked me if I would like that. I nodded and Mama smiled at me through her tears. Mama said she was glad. I kept wiping my face while she drove to the store. Mama came out with three paper wrapped vanilla ice cream cones. She handed me one first, and gave my dirty face a kiss. Then she handed one to Charlene and held one for Patricia to lick. Sometimes Mama took a lick because Patricia's cone was melting too fast.

On the way home Mama said after Patricia was down for her nap, we could help her make Gingerbread men cookies and put raisins in for eyes, nose, and a mouth, She said they should be done when Oleta got home from school and we could all have one. I was cheering up little by little. When we were making cookies Mama asked what I would have done when I got to the school door. I told her I would have knocked and waited for the teacher. I would tell her I wanted to find Oleta and sit with her.

Oleta arrived home just in time for a warm Gingerbread Man cookie. I told her I walked almost to her school to see her. She gasped and looked at Mama and she nodded and told her the story. Mama asked Oleta what she would have done if I had walked in the door. She said she would know I wasn't supposed to be there and would ask Mrs. Baker if she should walk me home. Mama was proud of her answer and told her that it would have been the right thing to do. She asked me how I knew to knock on the door. I told her that it is what we do when we go to people's houses if they don't see us first and have the door open. I also told Mama that I didn't know where to go when I got inside and the teacher would show me where my sister was. Mama smiled. She asked if I knew right away how to get to school. I told her I did because I knew it was a little farther than our church. She told me I have been really paying attention to things around me, adding that by next year she was sure I would like school and have fun learning lots of new things.

The whole incident must have seemed more like a dream to my mother than a reality. After Daddy learned what I did at the supper table, he called me a scamp and asked me if I would ever do it again. I shook my head. He told me when Mama says "No" I need to accept that the first time. I nodded. He patted me on the head, smiled and told me I was a nice girl and that Mama and Daddy love me. I liked that because Daddy was not often near us. He was usually working in the fields or in the barn. He didn't talk with me much. He listened to the news on the radio at night and we children were to be quiet.

When Christmas season finally came I went to the Christmas program with Mama and Charlene. Daddy stayed home with Patricia. I sat with Oleta and Charlene sat on Mama's lap. It was fun to see and hear the school kids when they were up front and spoke pieces and sang. The big Christmas tree was really beautiful. We never had one. Our house was too little. Both Charlene and I got a present. Mine was a small all black Mickey Mouse with a long tail. I thought it was licorice and tried to take a bite. Oleta said it was a toy. We both laughed. We had Christmas cookies and a candy cane to eat. Everyone seemed to have fun.

Soon it was Christmas Eve. We went to church for the Christmas Eve program. Oleta spoke a piece. Some people sang solos and some did a short play with baby Jesus in a manger. We had a pretty Christmas tree with no presents, but a bag of candy was handed out to all the children when church was over. I liked going to the program. After we were home from church we hung up our stockings on a chair we picked from a line of four. We didn't hang up anklets. We used Oleta's long socks. Mama put our name on each sock and chair. Just as we were ready for bed we heard a tap at our bedroom window and looked and saw Santa's face at the window. He ducked out of sight fast. Mama said he was probably just checking to see if we were ready for bed. We had sat out a cookie and glass of milk for Santa Claus. We went right to bed after seeing Santa at the window.

We were up early Christmas morning. Mama told us the night before we had to wait until Daddy was done with the milking and he would call us when we could come out of our bedroom to see what Santa brought. We were ready and waiting when he called us. I immediately saw the doll buggy I wanted so much. I jumped up and down and clapped my hands in glee. It was big enough to take my rag doll for a ride just like I wanted. There was a new fuzzy pair of pink pajamas on the seat of my chair. I had two boxes of Cards. One was words and pictures. The other was numbers and pictures. My sock had a box of Cracker Jacks and a big orange that we almost never got to eat. There was a small box of raisins, a chocolate Santa wrapped in pretty foil and three big bubble gums. All of us older three children had the same things in our socks. Each one had different presents on or next to their chair, except we all had new pajamas. Everybody was really happy with their nice presents. There was a bowl of nuts in the shell on the table and a smaller one of Christmas candies. The cookie was gone and the empty glass was on the table. We were glad Santa liked his treat.

Daddy had a new red plaid wool shirt and Mama had a new baby blue dress. Daddy said he was going to save his nice shirt and wear a white one for Christmas day at Mama's parent's house. He said since Mama had a pretty dress to wear, he had better look dressed up, too. Mama had made all of us girls new dresses for the Christmas season. We three older girls wore ours to the school and church Christmas programs. We were all going to wear our new dresses for going to Grandma and Grandpas for Christmas. My dress was green with a full skirt. I loved to twirl in it. It had a white collar and wide white belt that tied in back with a big bow. It was the prettiest dress I had ever had. I was wearing Oleta's black patent leather church shoes because they didn't fit her, still looked new and fit me. Mama had to buy Oleta new ones before Christmas. Charlene wore mine. Patricia wore hand-me-down white hard soled baby shoes, but she had a new pretty dress. She was fourteen months old. She liked her little rubber dolly Santa brought and kept chewing on its fingers and toes. She carried it around with her blanket. Christmas was an expensive time of year for Mama and Daddy. We never did much for birthdays so this was the big family expense of the year. The memories I hold of Christmas during our growing up years even in the throes of the great depression are happy ones for me. I owe it all to my parents for making it such a wonderful experience.

Chapter 10

Money Crisis

We children had no real concept of the devastation the depression caused so many in America. We knew our parents didn't have a lot of money to spend, but thought that was just how life was.

By fall, after all the crops were harvested and all sold that weren't needed for the animals, the terrible truth was that there was not enough money to pay Grandpa and Grandma the expected amount for the year. Crop prices had dropped too low and living costs for the family had increased. It was a terrible blow to my parents. The humiliation alone was very painful. They were very concerned how Daddy's parents would deal with the situation. The day they met for discussion of the situation was very uncomfortable. Daddy defended the couple having four children in such bad times, but his parents were empathetic and knew he needed a boy and Daddy didn't marry young. Their understanding was a big relief. Daddy's father offered to rescue my parents by taking one half of the crop production each year until they could meet the original payments on the contract they both signed. At that time the original contract would resume. Grandpa still wanted the contract to be paid in full by the set time. He was determined it was the only responsible way for his son to deal with his financial situation. He reminded my father that if he had dealt with a bank he would be losing the farm. Daddy said he was well aware that would be the case and thanked his father. Daddy was forced to accept the offer. There was no other. It was a scary thought to know the family would now be living off fifty acres instead of a hundred. Things needed to change fast regarding the economy as the crops weren't bringing in enough from one-hundred acres.

Now there were six mouths to feed plus other expenses in raising their children. Both my parents were experiencing a feeling of panic. They could see no way of cutting expenses anywhere. Daddy had been repairing equipment that really needed replacing, but there was no money for that. Replacement was out of the question just as it was building the big house. They were stuck in the tiny one with no idea how long it would be. Mama was very disappointed and Daddy likely felt humiliated. Their financial situation looked very bleak. They had to have faith that things would turn around. For some consolation, they told themselves they were still better off than many people. Daddy still had work and the family had a roof over their heads. My parents tried to be positive.

Daddy had his own ideas of where the government went wrong. People all over were blaming President Calvin Coolidge for the mess. There was no use wasting time thinking about what may have been. They needed to concentrate on overcoming their dire situation. It seems only natural that my parents both must have had the thought cross their mind in wondering what they would be experiencing if Daddy had become a history professor. History would continue to be taught and teachers needed.

I expect my mother thought if they were where God wanted them to be, He would surely bring them through as long as they continued their intention to overcome a seemingly insurmountable adversity. I am not as sure that Daddy saw it that way, but he may have. I think he would have felt that God honored his consideration for his father in staying in farming where he could be of help to him. We had more sources of food available than most farmers as we had the nice orchard, vineyard, and honey bees. Garden and berry patches were common for farmers. Ours was a wonderful source of healthy food. We could nearly live off the land as we had eggs, milk, and sometimes beef and pork available. Daddy knew how to butcher, prepare, and cure meats, was a good fisherman and hunter and had a good understanding of mechanics relating to farm implements as well as understanding agriculture. He surely understood various woods and carpentry and was willing to learn what he didn't know about building a nice house. Not much daunted him. Both he and Mama were very grateful they owned a tractor and car free and clear. Five months after he and Mama were married, he paid off his brother for his share in the car.

Daddy was fortunate in that somehow there was enough money for him to buy a tractor without a loan soon after marriage. The depression was a sudden and shocking change in the economy almost overnight. Until then Daddy was prospering. Our family made it through the winter with good health, food, and their needs met. Daddy had done considerable hunting for raccoons, rabbits, squirrels, and deer in the late fall and early winter. His successes supplied some extra money from pelts he sold and extra meat for the family. Daddy had cut and stacked plenty of wood for the cold months to keep us warm and provide wood for the cook stove. There wasn't much money for Christmas, but our parents saw to it that Santa came with some nice little presents as there wasn't room for anything of much size.

In the spring and summer my parents worked like slaves. I remember Mama being at the clothesline quite often where she had Dutch cheese in the making. She added crushed rennet tablets to milk; they are rennin enzymes from calf's stomachs. The tablets caused the milk to sour and coagulate. After the mixture sat awhile and became thick and chunky, Mama put it in a cheesecloth and hung it on the line. She would gently squeeze the contents and the whey ran into a pail that she placed on the ground underneath. Every few minutes she would squeeze the bag full of cheese to try to get all the whey out of the cheese. The whey would be fed to the pigs after it was mixed in with other items like potato peelings and other things pigs ate. Between Daddy's hunting dog, the cats, and the pigs nothing went to waste. Mama told her children that Dutch cheese was what Little Miss Muffet ate, and then repeated the poem that said she was eating her curds and whey. We all ate the cheese very heartily.

Mama was nobody's fool. I can remember many times in the mid afternoon when we children were playing outside and were so hungry that Mama had us wash our hands really well and made us each a ball of the cottage cheese that had become a little dry. We took it outside and ate it, barely losing an ort. It was so good. Sometimes when we were hungry, Mama would give us a little fresh sauerkraut from the crock. Mama had made it and it was good as were the dill pickles that she made. Mama would sometimes tell us we could each have one; but only after we had scrubbed our hands very clean.

In the winter, the pickles were very crunchy as they had little ice crystals in them. The salt brine kept them from freezing hard. They were the best dill pickles I have ever eaten. Mama sometimes served sauerkraut with slim slices of Daddy's homemade summer sausage in it. She often served her homemade Dutch cheese with that meal and topped it off with applesauce with cinnamon. The most often served meal, after the garden stopped production, was navy bean soup with bacon pieces in it. We liked dipping homemade bread in it even if it wasn't really fresh. When the bread supply was low Mama made cornmeal bread and it was good. Mama always managed to find something to fix for meals for her big family.

We all seemed to be healthy. Back then they didn't do cholesterol tests. Our diet often contained pork because it was fairly easy and quite economical to raise. With no refrigeration it could be preserved without canning. Beef needed to be canned and was a huge job as it came in a larger quantity than pork. Mama was just too busy to get it done immediately while the meat was still fresh.

Oleta was becoming a school girl by September. Mama made her dresses and underskirts whenever she found time. It usually meant sacrificing sleep and sewing at night after her children were all in bed. It was not easy to do as she had to do it during canning season and Mama was very tired after a long hard day of work.

Mama ordered fabric remnants that were sold at a good price. They were sold as a bundle with guaranteed yardage of each piece and the pattern was sold as plaids or small flowers or other designs that denoted they were suitable for children of a certain age range. The colors were never known, but the type of fabric was. Mama bought cotton as it was washable; she hoped it wouldn't be terrible stuff to iron. Mama bought sturdy soft white fabric for underskirts. She could make them quickly as they had only a neck hole and arm holes that needed binding and a skirt with a little flair attached to a bodice. They were hemmed by the sewing machine. She made her own pattern after using Oleta's church dress for size along with taking her body measurements. She made her clothes as large as she dared so they would fit as long as possible. The dresses were all the same style, but with different trim and some with white collars instead of the same as the dress fabric. She made each dress appear different. Sometimes she styled the sleeves differently. Other times she put in a contrasting color for the yoke. The popular style was a deep yoked short bodice. The material for the lower part of the dress was shirred for some fullness Mama was very creative and sewed well. She could make much nicer dresses for much less than the ones in the catalogs. When printed cotton feed bags were available, the homemade dresses cost almost nothing.

Ordering remnants was very inexpensive, very practical and Oleta was thrilled with her new dresses and underskirts. Mama had made out a big order from the *Sears Roebuck* and *Montgomery Ward* catalogs for Oleta's other school items. She ordered a cardigan, a package of six panties, a six pair pack of anklets, six pairs of beige toned long cotton stockings that were still too warm for school, but could change any time. She made garters from elastic for holding up the long stockings. Oleta would soon need a warm jacket. Mama ordered her a two piece wool snowsuit, with matching mittens and a hat with a strap under the chin. Oleta picked maroon as the color she liked best from the selection. It took a lot of measurements to send in with the order as required for determining the correct clothing sizes.

To order shoes, Oleta stood on paper while Mama drew around her foot. That was sent in to determine her shoe size. Mama ordered her brown high tops and galoshes. The shoes seemed like they were sturdy and durable and Mama hoped would last through the school year even with all the trips to school and home and their use on the playground. She ordered Oleta a lunchbox, crayons, tablet, pencils, a big eraser, and blunt scissors. Oleta was very excited. Our parents were getting a sample of what lay ahead of them for many years. When the packages came in the mail Oleta could barely wait to see all her new things. We other two children gathered around as Oleta picked up and looked over what came in the orders. Patricia was in her crib so the orders were opened in our children's tiny bedroom where the clothes would be hung and stored and where Honey could see them too. We all stood in awe at what she had acquired. There were more things than we saw at Christmas.

After Oleta saw everything and clothes were being put away in Oleta's and my top drawer of the chest of drawers, I picked up her lunch pail and looked at Mickey Mouse and Mini Mouse on it. I said I really liked it. Mama told Oleta she could not use any of her things until she went to school, but told her she could open her color box and see what colors were inside it. I craned my neck to see them. There was red, yellow, green, blue, black, and brown. Mama saw my excitement and said next school year it would be my turn to get lots of nice new things. I clapped my hands and jumped for joy. Oleta put all her school items that weren't clothes in her lunch pail. Mama took it to the kitchen and put it on top of the green cabinet in the kitchen. She would wrap Oleta's lunch well in waxed paper and Oleta could carry all her items except her tablet in her lunch box her first day of school.

After seeing all of Oleta's new dresses hanging with her cardigan and snowsuit, I had fun trying to decide which of her dresses I liked best. Oleta said she liked them all and could hardly wait to start school. She loved books and could read many words and say her ABCs and do some addition and subtraction before she started school. I was learning them, too, but in shorter sessions than Oleta studied them.

Mama told me when Oleta started school she wanted me to sleep on the bottom with Charlene until Friday and Saturday nights. Then, if I wanted to sleep in bed with Oleta I could. I found it fun to climb the ladder to get to the top bunk so slept with Oleta on those nights. I liked the idea of sleeping both places as did Charlene. Mama knew I was a live wire and she wanted Oleta to get a good night's sleep on school days.

Patricia's crib was under the rod of clothes, but the clothes were on just one end away from her crib. The end over her crib had toys hanging from it to entertain Honey. We sometimes played in our bedroom so she could see us. She was a sweet baby.

Oleta, wearing her new clothes, looked nice her first day of school. Her hair was cut very short including her bangs. She had a high forehead that wouldn't be well covered. Only a few days before school started, she got the shears out of the kitchen drawer and butchered her hair. Mama did her best to make it look presentable and it was quite passable though very short. It would soon grow so only a minor problem in Oleta's eyes. After that, Mama kept her shears on top of the green cabinet and out of reach from children.

School was all that Oleta expected. She really liked it. She told me of the fun she had on the teeter-totter and swings. None of us had ever been on either so it sounded very exciting to me. I anticipated going to school the next fall. My parents were determined that one way or other they would send me out the door for school in presentable looking clothes and needed school items.

Chapter 11

Midnight

Spring came early this year. It was unusually warm on Easter Sunday. We children were up early and anxious to find a small Easter basket outside with our name on it. Patricia's basket was easy to find. It hung on the pump handle. We older children knew we were not to tell if we found someone else's basket. It wasn't long before each of us found our own. Each basket had some cream filled big eggs. There were several different colors of jelly beans, three yellow marshmallow chicks with orange beaks, and a big hollow chocolate bunny on the top of all the grassy decoration and goodies.

Mama took us to church Easter Sunday. Everyone except Patricia wore Christmas dresses for Easter. She wore one of the little dresses that were left from ones Charlene once wore because her Christmas dress didn't fit anymore. We had a nice dinner at Grandma and Grandpa's house. It was fun to go there.

It was warm enough outside that Mama said we could go barefooted. We loved that. We had to change clothes first. Mama thought if we were barefoot we would stay outside and play longer and not desire to eat too much candy. She was always thinking ahead.

I took my doll buggy outside and put the big fat black cat I called Midnight in my buggy. I put my doll's dress on her and she didn't seem to mind; she seemed to like riding in the buggy. We always had cats around, usually in the barn catching mice. Sometimes on warm sunny days they liked being in the sun near the house. Daddy's dog was friendly, but he liked Daddy best and liked it in the shade on warm days. Mama didn't much like cats. She was never mean to them; she just didn't want them in the house. She did keep a dish outside the laundry room for a few orts for them. Oleta and Charlene were playing with the wagon. Mama snapped a few pictures of us from her trusty Kodak camera. She took a close up picture of Midnight in my buggy wearing a dress. Mama was so pleased I

66

wasn't afraid of cats and dogs after the traumatic event I had experienced. She chuckled to herself, thinking, *Not even black ones.*

During the night after Easter day a fierce thunderstorm moved in. The lightning was snapping all around and the thunder that followed was almost deafening. The rain was heavily pouring down. Despite all the noise, Mama thought she heard a cat meowing very loudly. She thought she heard it several times. Maybe it was a frightened child. She got up to investigate. As she walked near the dining room window closest to the washroom, she heard a frantic cry. She slid up the bottom window and there was Midnight soaking wet. She had given birth to kittens in the bushel basket that was on its side in the corner between the dining and washroom walls on the outside of the house. Water was coming in the basket and the kittens were about to drown. Midnight grabbed a kitten by the nape of the neck and jumped through the open window. Mama reached out and grabbed two more. The mama cat rushed back for the last one. Mama made sure there were only four. Though soaking wet herself, she pulled down the window and quickly ran for a bath towel and spread it out and put the kittens on it and dried off the mother cat that was busy trying to lick her kittens dry. The poor little things were shivering. Mama went quickly and grabbed a second towel and placed it on the floor in the corner. She pulled the mama cat and her babies over to it and Mama put the babies on a dry towel. Their mama walked on the towel and wrapped her body around her kittens. She looked up at Mama, gave her wet arm a lick as if in great appreciation. Mama was in tears; she felt so sorry for the awful experience Midnight and her kittens had just gone through.

Mama went in the kitchen and washed her arms and dried them and went into her children's bedroom to see who was whimpering. She didn't tell us about Midnight. Her philosophy that some things are just better left unsaid applied to the situation well. She wanted us to get back to sleep as we were all awake. She told us she would read us a story. She sat on the floor between the bed and crib with her back against the chest of drawers. The lightning was so frequent she could see to read with no problem. Sometimes the thunder cracked so loud the children didn't hear what she said. It didn't really matter. Mama just wanted us to sleep. She told us she would stay in the room until the storm let up and we were asleep. It wasn't long before Mama was back in bed.

In the morning the children had a big surprise. There was Midnight in the corner with four little kittens. I yelled out that there was one a piece for each of us children. Mama offered a cautious smile. She said she would feed the Mama cat some warm milk and after breakfast was over she would take the cat family to the barn and fix them a little house. She said we could go with her if we were dressed. It didn't take us long to get dressed. Oleta didn't go because she had to walk to school, but the rest of us did. Mama found a box and cut a small door in it just big enough for Midnight to get through. She sat it upside down over a nice thick pile of straw. First she put a large folded rag on the straw and put the kittens in their cozy little house. Their mama came right in with them and snuggled up to them. She purred like she was singing to them. We all walked away together. Mama said Daddy would give her some warm milk when he milked the cows. She said mama cats don't always like people around their new kittens so not to go see them until she took us with her. Mama was well aware that warning needed saying. She told us Midnight would spend most of her time with the kittens while they were still little, but if she came to the house she said she would find something to feed her. It seems Mama had a tender spot for this cat family. She knew she had spared a disaster for them. She told me she was really pleased I took the dress off her after I was done playing with her. She said I did the right thing and must always remember to do it every time I dress up a cat. She sort of swallowed a little chuckle. Mama didn't tell us the reason she put the box over the cat family and made such a narrow door was to keep a tom cat from killing the kittens as they sometimes do. She told herself again that some things are best left unsaid.

Chapter 12

Struggling

Summer of 1937 was busy as ever. I was soon going to start school. Mama was busy making Oleta and me some dresses and underskirts. She made five for Oleta three for me as I could wear some of hers from last school year. None of them fit her anymore and some were worn out from playing in them at home. This year the catalog school orders would be bigger than the one a year ago. We both needed new snowsuits, hats, and mittens. Oleta's were worn out, the cuffs and linings of her jacket and pants had worn through. Her high tops were worn out. She needed a new cardigan and hers fit me. We both needed new shoes and she needed new galoshes. Mama ordered us new panties and stockings. Oleta had some anklets left we could both wear. I was getting a new lunch box and school supplies. Oleta was going to use her same lunch box again. I picked out a green snowsuit set and Oleta chose dark red. When our new things came in the mail it was so much fun and everything fit right.

Oleta and I walked to school together. Sometimes we walked with two other girls who lived near us. I liked school a lot. It was really fun. My sister and I played on the teeter-totter together sometimes and in the swings, too. Sometimes I sat on her lap facing her and we had lots of good laughs. It was fun swinging up high. One day when I was looking for her one of the big boys grabbed me and shut me in the woodshed. He pulled the wood piece across the door so I couldn't open it. He was always getting in trouble at school and the teacher often scolded him. Sometimes she made him do his school work all over. I didn't know if anybody saw him put me in the shed so I waited for him to let me out. I knew it was so noisy on the playground that nobody could hear me if I yelled. I started to cry. This was our short recess and I knew the bell would soon ring and my sister would see I was missing and tell the teacher, but I couldn't stop crying. Suddenly I heard the door lock slide move and the door opened. The mean boy saw me crying and ran. I found my sister and told her what happened. She was very surprised. I told her I didn't tell the teacher. She said most of the school kids were nice. I told her I was afraid of him. She said to just stay away from him and we will tell Mama when we get home because she will know what to do.

When we were home we told Mama. She said for Oleta to keep an eye on me at recesses and if it happened again to tell the teacher. Mama told me she was pretty certain the troublemaker would not be in school the next year. She advised that since I know he does naughty things, to keep track of where he is, keep my distance from him and ignore him .I soon became comfortable and played mainly with a girl in my class and Oleta played with a girl in her class and finally two after another girl joined her class.

The wood shed stored pieces of wood to help get the fire going in the morning before adding coal from the coal bin that was near the furnace. On Mondays an old man next door to the school got the fire going before the teacher arrived. There was a girl's and boy's cloakroom in the school house. Each had a small enclosed area with a sink and toilet. We hung our outerwear on a long row of hooks in the big area of the room. We left out boots beneath them.

In the winter, the kids brought washed raw potatoes to school and at the ten thirty recess, marked their initials on them with chalk and put them on the top of the furnace. By noon they smelled wonderful and we all ate baked potatoes with butter and salt we had in our lunchboxes. Sometimes we might have a piece of meat with them or maybe a boiled egg and a cookie. In the warmer months we had peanut butter sandwiches, carrots or tomato, and fresh fruit. Sometimes we had a butter and mustard sandwich, or mayonnaise sandwich with a boiled egg and a tomato or long sliced cucumber, and some kind of fruit. Once in a while we had potted meat. It was like finely ground ham made into a spread. The cans were small and Mama spread it thin. Amazingly, we never became sick from salmonella. It was probably because we started back to school in September when weather was beginning to cool. If we ever had a bologna sandwich it was a very rare treat. I always had to have one big bite at the ten thirty recess. It was just too hard to wait until noon.

With no refrigeration in our home it was hard to keep meats like bologna fresh for long. Sometimes we would have a slice of Daddy's homemade summer sausage in our lunch, but Mama usually fried it for our supper meal. During these depression years a bread truck with day-old breads, tiny pies, little cakes, and cookies ran in rural areas. Daddy met the truck a few miles away and loaded up on things that were cheaper than Mama could make. Once in a while he would find cream-filled wafer cookies, double cakes of chocolate with a cream filling inside, and pink marshmallow puffy round top covered with coconut. Those items were so special in our lunch boxes it seemed like Christmas.

Our meals at home were almost always very basic. Sometimes we had fried mush when we had no meat. It was made from cornmeal and water that cooked it until thickened. Then it was poured into a baking pan and cooled until it was firm enough to slice and fry. Mama always saved the bacon fat and used it for frying certain foods. It made the mush taste good. She often served it with navy bean soup. When we didn't have meat, Mama sometimes made cod fish gravy. Small cod fish fillets were dried and salted and came in a wooden box with a slide lid. Mama took a few pieces out of the box and soaked them in water and rehydrated them and took out much of the salt. She poured milk in a pan and added the fish pieces she had cut into small pieces. She stirred in a smooth flour and milk thickening to make the gravy. Mama usually served it with boiled potatoes. If there were enough left, she would chop them and fry them in the morning and serve them to Daddy with his soft fried eggs and pancakes.

We didn't often have toast as it was not easy to make on the stove top as the heat couldn't be regulated. She made Daddy pancakes almost every morning as he always wanted to eat something he said stuck to his ribs and wanted us to do so too. I was not keen on pancakes because I always thought they stuck more to the top of my mouth than my ribs. None of us were obese or even close to being considered fat.

In the winter months when we were young, Mama often made us children oatmeal that we sweetened with honey and sometimes added cinnamon for flavor. In the warm weather we often ate Wheaties. Even back then it was called the Breakfast of Champions. I think it was the cereal that contained a free cereal bowl with a black strip near the top in each box. Sometimes Mama made French toast when the bread was getting stale. She used stale bread for making bread pudding, too. We could not afford to be wasteful. That has stuck with me all my life. It really bothers me to see people waste food or anything.

When we had fresh garden vegetables Mama often fixed boiled dinner made from potatoes, cabbage, carrots, onions, and sometimes put in a peeled turnip cut in half for Daddy as the rest of us were not fond of the strong taste. Mama added pieces of home-cured ham which added salt and the good meat flavor. Sometimes we had macaroni and stewed tomatoes as a meal. We ate to live instead of lived to eat. Our suppers were sometimes green fried tomatoes and corn on the cob; I loved that meal. Sometimes we had fried potatoes and corn. Mama made some of the potatoes with onions and some plain; I liked the ones with onions. They made the house smell like the fair. When we had fresh peas Mama made them with tiny potatoes in a creamy sauce. Daddy liked what he called rivvels but Mama had never heard of them. He told her they were made like homemade noodles, but were dropped in small pieces into a pea and milk combination instead of being rolled out and sliced like noodles. The rivvels thickened the milk into a sauce. We liked them.

Many of our meals did not include meat, and when they did, it was in conservative amounts. Mama often fixed deviled eggs that were always a hit. We ate almost anything put in front of us; it was eat or go hungry and I was always hungry. There were two things I just could hardly get down my gullet. One was apple butter, a brownish spicy spread. The other was even worse. It was canned strawberries that had become mushy and pale pink and did not even come close to looking or tasting like a strawberry. I am afraid I would have to be starving to death to get one down even today. I loved fresh ones.

Mama worked many hours preparing food for our family. So many times when she worked at canning or fixing meals or even ironing, the tiny kitchen was way too warm for her comfort. It was common to see beads of perspiration on her face. I never remember hearing her complain, but I do remember seeing her wipe her perspiration on her apron. In the spring Mama dug up dandelion greens, cleaned them well and fixed a large kettle full for a meal. She and Daddy put vinegar and salt and pepper on theirs. We children only used a little butter and salt. They were a special treat. We often had them with fried potatoes. I remember when I saw her and thought she was lonely, I would catch up with her and hang on her free hand while the others who were near would walk with us. Little did we consider it probably was a nice time for her peace and quiet. She carried a big pail and a hand spade and dug them up until the pail was full and went back to the house to clean them. It seemed nothing she did was ever easy.

There were times we didn't eat homemade butter because we needed to sell all the milk for money. We used oleomargarine that came in a box and was white with a small packet of orange coloring in it. Mama would open the margarine, let it soften in a bowl and then mix in the coloring until it was well blended. It looked like butter and was much cheaper. When we had corn on the cob and used butter, Daddy would salt it so much that we could only tolerate a little on our corn. He never mentioned it, but we knew. It was awful if we were too generous on our application. After the first ear we learned what not to do.

I remember one butchering day when Grandma came over with Grandpa to help Mama clean the small intestines of the hog for sausage casings. She made the best canned sausage I have ever eaten. The meat was equally shared between the two families and Grandpa came to help Daddy butcher. It was not a simple job. The hog was castrated when a young pig so the meat would be tender and have a good flavor. Grandpa always helped with that procedure. A tub was under the dead pig that Daddy shot. It was strung up by the hind legs with pulleys so the men could gut it out and have the inside waste parts drop in a tub under it. The hide was singed with a blow torch. Then the pig was lowered into a large barrel of very hot water that prepared the hide for scraping. After the small intestines were separated from the lower intestines they were put in a pail of cold water and rinsed. They sat in a fresh pail of water while Grandma and Mama sat outside facing each other with a square board on their lap and cut the intestines into twelve inch long pieces. They scraped them out by using a heavy butcher knife that they held in such a way that it wouldn't cut the intestine but put enough pressure on it to squeeze out the contents. They were washed through many pails of fresh water and taken to the house. I never saw either Mama or Grandma grimace at the most sickening smell imaginable; they just did what they needed to do. To this day if I even hear the words of natural casings mentioned, that awful odor is so well instilled in my mind that I need to dispense of the thought as soon as possible for my own well-being and those of anyone near me.

It amazes me I can't seem to get beyond that as I gladly ate the sausage that was in the natural casings when I was young. Natural casing hotdogs never are in my shopping cart. Grandma stayed and helped Mama make the sausage and stuff it in the casings that were cut into two inch pieces. These were put into wide mouthed canning jars with a little hot water poured over them. The sealed jars were placed in the copper boiler for a hot water bath canning method. It was tricky to keep the water boiling for a given length of time on a wood stove. The pig's liver was divided before our grandparents left with the rest of their meat. It was certain that we and they would be having fried liver and onions for supper with fried potatoes. Liver was always the first meat eaten. Our grandparents had an ice box so they could save part of the liver for a second day. Nothing worthwhile is ever easy to accomplish. How well our parents and those before them knew it.

Chapter 13

Frozen to Death

One calm very cold winter night Daddy took his dog Lead hunting with him in our woods. Daddy was hunting for raccoons that were getting in our cornfield and ruining some of the corn. Daddy sold the pelts and we ate the meat. Hunting them served three good purposes. Daddy almost always was successful when he went hunting.

Lead was distracted during their hunt and went after a fox. He chased it out of the woods and into a big brush pile on our neighbor's property. Daddy could not see the dog or fox and finally came home without the dog as Lead was insistent he get the fox. He was barking so much that he apparently didn't hear Daddy call him. Fox killed the pheasants and chickens so Daddy didn't want them around and he didn't mind if the dog got rid of it. Daddy was cold and came back to the house carrying a dead raccoon. The dog had helped Daddy get one by treeing it. He expected the dog would track him home and eventually come back. Daddy went to bed after a cup of hot coffee. He knew when his hunting companion returned that he would be at the back door barking to be let inside. Daddy would hear him and let him in the wash room.

By the time Daddy got up to milk the cows, his dog had not returned home. That had never happened and Daddy became concerned. After breakfast was over Daddy went out looking for his dog. He went back to the brush pile and looked everywhere in the area. The wind had come up and blew the snow that covered the tracks. Daddy just could not imagine where his dog would be. He thought the fox may have led the dog on a longer chase and the dog would eventually come home. As Daddy followed the fence row that would lead back to the lane, he spotted something in the fence. It was a short distance ahead of him. The closer he came, the more it looked like Lead; it was. The poor dog had become caught in the fence as he tried to jump it. He had chewed his tail nearly off trying to get free.

Daddy reached out to touch him, but he was dead and frozen stiff. It was a terrible shock for Daddy who had lost his friend and hunting companion. As soon as Mama saw his face she knew something sad had occurred. Daddy told her the story and Mama was very sad, too. Daddy repeated that he should never have left the dog, but Mama told him he had always come home before and in this case it was the practical thing for Daddy to do. She poured two cups of coffee and through two pairs of teary eyes they each drank a cup of coffee together.

After the coffee was gone, Daddy said he would go back and bury the dog if the ground wasn't too hard. We children were in school and were glad we didn't have to see our parents feeling so sad. We had already seen Daddy bury one other dog that a car hit and killed. I still remember how sad it was. I remember Daddy placing the dog's long ear over its eye to keep the dirt out of it. A Mennonite man had hit the dog. Some time later he came to the house to confess to Daddy and told him he was sorry. He asked forgiveness for not telling Daddy right away; Daddy forgave him.

Our parents didn't keep things from us that were not of their personal and private lives. They were both realistic about life and death when we were old enough to understand. We were not sheltered in that sense. They were careful how they spoke to us and never disparaged us. We knew they expected us to do well in school and we did. They told us we had good brains and were capable of achieving good grades in school. Mama taught us to be kind to our siblings and be good to others.

Our parents realized in rural school we had little choice in close friends. We weren't picked on, but we knew we were different in the eyes of the Mennonites and that was a little hard to deal with sometimes being a minority in school. They all knew each other and their families. We knew only the ones who lived near our home. They understood their religion but not ours. As we grew older in rural school we felt they saw us as inferior to them in religion and lifestyle. They started out with large homes and we didn't. It was easier to keep a house tidy when there was space for everything. They often had several adult females in the home at one time. At that time they didn't go to school beyond the eighth grade when the young men stayed home and helped with farm work and the young ladies lived at home and helped the family with work until they married. With large families, there was plenty of help with sewing, baking, cooking, gardening, cleaning and doing laundry and ironing so they had an advantage in keeping their houses clean and themselves always neat in appearance. The older ones helped keep their younger siblings neat and clean.

Mama and Daddy's situation was different. For many years, our parents had little help so we didn't seem to quite measure up to them. Mama reminded us that they were by far the minority in the county, we just happened to live in a Mennonite community. She said they were good people who viewed religion different from us. She told us to remember we had the same right to have our own religion as they did. Mama explained she understood that there was not the same understanding between us and our present school friends, but to make the most of our relationships. She added that in high school it would be different. When we had the opportunity in high school she advised us to pick our best friends with care. We were taught to be honest, to behave respectably and to be polite to everyone. If we found our high school friends were not the kind of people we were, she suggested we seek others that were more of like intelligence and moral standards. She made it clear she did not mean for us to snub classmates, but to be kind but not create a close friendship with them. She taught us if any treated us in a less than kind way the problem was with them. She said to pray for them instead of feeling hostile towards them and we might be surprised at the outcome. Mama explained that since we didn't know their parents we had no idea what their home life was like. Maybe it was not a good environment. She said the reason a person picks on or shuns someone else is due to their own inward unhappiness or poor upbringing. She said she expected us to have many good friends. It was her way to leave things on a positive note.

I think she realized that going to high school where we didn't know the other students would be challenging. Some of them had known each other most of their lives and probably already had their cliques. She knew as long as we were in the little house we couldn't invite anyone to come home with us for overnight. One reason was lack of room and the other might be embarrassment. As she was a person who always thought ahead, I am sure she very much wanted us to be in our big house by the time we started high school. I am sure she said many prayers for her children. She was very aware of our needs.

While we were all still in rural school, we had school projects where students were asked to sell garden or flower seeds to make money for the project. On our way home from school we walked past a place we always considered very spooky. An old spinster who lived there seldom communicated with anyone. She had red hair tied back with ringlets hanging down the back of her neck. We always thought of her as the witch that Hansel and Gretel encountered. It took courage to stop at her house. It was a dark place with bare wood floors that squeaked when anyone walked on them. The thing that scared us most was that she always locked the doors right behind us after inviting us inside. She never offered us a place to sit. She just stood in the kitchen which was the room we entered. Not one of us would have gone to her house alone. I don't recall she ever bought a thing from us. Our parents felt she knew who we were, but she didn't act that way. She said very little to us. Her demeanor was very peculiar and aloof. We were all glad to say we needed to get home and saw and heard the door unlock. Many years later our mother picked her up and took her to church with her. She did go for some time, but I was no longer living at home. She looked very old the last time I saw her. I do know that I was very surprised she went to church with Mother. How quickly we judge people sometimes and how wrong our judgment often is. We don't like taking blame.

Not wanting to take blame reminds me of a story that is a mystery to me today. We girls had an imaginary acquaintance we created as our scapegoat. She wasn't nice. We named her Allie Ganger; I have no idea where the name came from as we never knew anybody with that first or last name. Long after I married, I established a clothing store for women and one day a lady walked in and bought some items. When she paid me she wrote me a check with her name on it and with a bank guarantee card. I nearly keeled over when I saw she had the exact first and last name as the girl we had created in our minds. I didn't mention a word about it to my customer, but I wonder if she heard my gasp. It was the only time she was ever in the store in the nine years I had it. As soon as she left I called my older sister and told her. She was as shocked as I was. It was probably the strangest event of my life.

Chapter 14

The Fair

The two biggest events of the year for us children were Christmas and the Gratiot County fair held at Ithaca. On children's day all the rides were only twenty-five cents. Mama was taking her four children to the fair so she fixed Daddy's noon meal ahead of time. We were each going to have a hotdog, a bun and a bottle of soda pop. We had only tasted pop once or twice before.

Mama said that after we left the fair she would take us to the dairy where they had bigger and better ice cream cones for less money than at the fair. We clapped our hands in sheer joy and great excitement. She knew with that in the plans she would have no problem with us wanting to stay at the fair longer than she wanted to endure. She was always thinking ahead.

We were so excited we could barely wait to get to the fair. It was ten o'clock in the morning when we arrived; lots of people already there. Mama suggested we go to the Merry-Go-Round first as Patricia could ride on that ride with Mama standing beside her. She said maybe she wouldn't want to ride on some we did. We were happy to go. As we stood in line waiting for Mama to buy our tickets, Mama reached in for her money she had put in her deep pocket of her dress. She left her purse locked in the trunk of the car as she wanted one hand free for hanging on Patricia's hand. Sometimes she would need both hands for getting tickets and food. She reached in a second time and the money was not there. Mama let out a big gasp. She double-checked both pockets and no money. Only a handkerchief was there. She was stunned. She said we needed to go back quickly to the car to see if there was any chance she had dropped it there. We met lots of people along the way. We all watched the ground as we tried to take the same route back to the car as we used before. We looked all around the car and Mama even rechecked her purse and inside the trunk. No money was found. She had no money in her purse. Mama was frantic. She just didn't know what to do. She stood staring and was probably praying. The tears were running down her face. We children were all wiping away tears. I remember well how badly I felt for her and all of us.

Suddenly Mama spotted a man who occasionally helped Daddy. She said to stay right with her and she would try to catch up with him. He was a bachelor and she thought maybe he would have extra money with him. She called his name, caught his attention and met up with him. With tears in her eyes she explained what had happened. We were all trying to wipe away our tears. Hugh immediately reached in his wallet and pulled out a twenty dollar bill and handed it to Mama. Mama gasped. She asked if he was sure he could loan her that much. He said Daddy had been good to him and he would be glad to do it. Mama told him they would get the money to him by the weekend. He said all he wanted was ten dollars. She responded by telling him that neither she nor her husband would feel right about that. He insisted, so she asked him to come for supper Saturday evening and they would pay him then. He smiled and agreed. Mama said she would never be able to tell him how much she appreciated what he had done. He told her if he had realized it was children's day and the busiest day at the fair he would have not been at the fair until tomorrow. He said he was glad he came today.

We all said," Thank you," in unison.

He gave a brief wave of the hand and walked away.

We hurried back to the Merry-Go-Round and were soon riding. Patricia rode a rooster and Mama stood beside her. We all had fun riding the creature we had picked. Mama had split the money between two pockets. She said she would try to keep one hand in her pocket when she could and with Patricia on the other side she didn't think a pickpocket could get to her money. She told us while we were in such a thick crowd she thinks that is what happened to the twenty dollar bill. She was feeling certain she had put it in her pocket.

Mama told us we could pick any ride we wanted. We picked the Tilt-A-Whirl next. We all went on it in the same seat. Mama held Patricia on her lap. Everyone found it lots of fun; we laughed the whole time. Next we saw the Octopus but Patricia didn't want to ride it and Mama was glad. Oleta, Charlene and I were eager; we found it scary fun. We held on tight. We laughed some of the time, but smiled a long time after our ride. The waiting lines were getting longer. We weren't able to rush on one ride after another.

We came to the Ferris wheel next. Mama and Patricia rode in one seat and the rest of us in another right behind them. I didn't like it when it stopped to let people off because our seat rocked and it felt like we could fall out. We decided it was not the most fun thing to ride, but we were glad we did.

Mama suggested since we were near the building that held 4-H exhibits and other exhibits that we go there. It was really fun. We saw goats and sheep we had never seen up close. There were some huge pigs and beautiful horses and huge scary bulls. We saw all kinds of rabbits up close, too. We had never been near live tame ones. They were so pretty with pink eyes. Next, we saw all kinds of chickens; we only had white ones at home called Leghorns. There were many different kinds on exhibit. Some were black and white sort of speckled ones, and some had beautiful iridescent feathers much like pheasants. There were some big ones with feathers almost all the way down their legs. Some really big roosters were there that seemed proud of themselves. One reminded me of the one that often followed Grandma to the house after she gathered eggs. It pecked at her stockings as she walked, but she paid no attention to it; I was afraid of it. There were turkeys, ducks and geese. Grandma had ducks and our relatives across from them had geese. Sometimes the geese chased people so we were careful around them when we went there.

Seeing the ducks reminded me of the story Daddy told us about the time he threw out fermented honey before he was married and still lived with his parents. His mother's ducks found it and ate it. Pretty soon they couldn't walk right and kept falling over. Daddy thought maybe they were all going to die. He knew they had eaten the honey so worried about them and held them up and gave them water. They were thirsty. They tried to fly, but crash landed. He thought he might soon be helping his unhappy mother can ducks for hours. Finally, he decided they were inebriated and went inside the house and got the camera and took pictures of them. Some were on their backs kicking their feet but none were standing. They started acting better after an hour. Daddy was feeling relieved that he was right. The ducks were, indeed, drunk. He decided he would tell Grandma when he had the pictures developed so he could show her. We have had many good laughs over that story. Nobody could tell it like Daddy. He said that after he showed the photos to his mother, she laughed, then asked him if he had any idea what he would have been doing if they all had died and he said he knew very well. She chuckled in her jolly way.

We got hungry looking at the nice pies, breads, and other good things on display. The 4-H girls had made them and were hoping to get a blue ribbon for the best one of each category. Mama suggested we go get our food and pop. We were beyond ready. She found a place for us to sit in the shade while we enjoyed our meal. We took our time eating and drinking our pop. Our fizzy soda pop sometimes brought tears to our eyes. It was impossible to drink fast. We asked to be pardoned for our burping. Mama laughed and told us we were pardoned. We really liked our meal and various flavored drinks. Mine was strawberry and so good.

Since Mama was done first, she suggested we go back for another ride or two after everyone was done eating all their meal. She knew the soda pop was a super special and fun drink. She told us we didn't have to try to rush, knowing we couldn't. We three older girls decided we wanted to go on the Loop-O-Plane. Mama wasn't too sure we would like it but we felt we would. After we got on and the ride started, we were scared stiff and our hands ached from hanging on tight. We were not screamers, but Mama could tell we were scared by looking at our faces. We didn't laugh until we got off the ride and it was because the ride was over. She asked if we wanted to ride it again, and when nobody did she chuckled. We discussed the ride as we walked. The two girls and I decided going backward in the ride was not as bad as forward. In the forward direction there were moments when we felt we were going to go straight down and slam into the ground. Sometimes we shut our eyes. It was undoubtedly a thrill. As we all interjected our thoughts, we could finally laugh heartily. We were still glad we had ridden on it, but had to admit Mama knew it was a very scary ride.

Patricia had spotted some little cars that went in a circle and little kids could pretend to steer which looked fun to her. She didn't want to sit alone and Mama asked Charlene if she wanted to go with her; she was very happy to. They had fun. After that ride Mama suggested one more ride. We all agreed on the Tilt-A Whirl. We thought it would be fun to all ride it together again. We laughed the entire time and still were laughing after we were off the ride. All of us agreed that by now an ice cream cone would taste good. The weather was beautiful, but we were getting a little too warm. We walked through the big crowd and Mama managed to finally get the car out of the big parking area. She drove straight to the ice cream parlor and we all picked out our favorite kind. I picked orange pineapple. We licked ice cream all the way home. We decided there was no better food treat in the world. We just couldn't quit talking about all the fun we had. It was a thrill beyond our description. At bedtime we thanked Mama for taking us when we kissed her goodnight. I said my usual last words to Mama. She always did as expected.

We didn't bother Daddy who was listening to the news as he concentrated with closed eyes. All of us told him some of the things we did and the wonderful time we had doing them. He was glad for us. We had thanked him for giving Mama the money so we could go. He was sad for us and Mama when she told him what had happened to the money. Daddy felt we were very fortunate in having seen Hugh. It is amazing how guardian angels work.

Chapter 15

Three Fires

One summer night we noticed the early evening sky had a red glow in the east. Daddy said something big was afire. It looked like it could be near our grandparent's home so we piled in the car and went to see what was burning. It was a relative's barn on the farm where they had their home and only an eighth of a mile past my grandparent's place.

As soon as we arrived at the fire Daddy ran to do what he could. The rest of us stood by the car Daddy had parked along the graveled road near the large lawn. He helped get animals and machinery out of the barn where it was possible. Men began driving from both directions and were running to help. A tractor and other machinery were removed from another storage shed. The fire was spreading fast because the hay in the mow was burning. The cattle had just been milked. Daddy and others quickly herded them out of the barn. Soon after we arrived the fire truck came. The men jumped out fast and went to work fighting the fire. Water was soon shooting at the fire. It was the first fire of its kind we children had ever seen and a very frightful scene. Huge sparks were flying all around.

After standing near our car for a while, Mama and us children saw several pigs running from the barn that were squealing because they had been burned. It was awful. They didn't seem to know where to go. The house was fairly close to the barn and it was feared that it may catch fire. The firemen occasionally sprayed the roof and side of the house as they fought the barn fire. The blaze was throwing sparks as far away as Daddy's parent's house. He ran down to their house and attached hoses together to keep the roof wet. There was nothing more he could do to help at his cousin's place so he climbed on the roof of his parent's house to watch for sparks as he watered it down. It was soon obvious the barn was not going to be saved and we just watched it burn down. It was several hours before our family went home.

Daddy stayed on the roof of Grandma and Grandpa's house until the fire truck left. It was late when we went to bed, but it was hard to go to sleep. I just couldn't get the terrible frightening sight out of my mind. I am sure it affected us all the same way. Even today seeing a night fire reminds me of the feeling I had when I watched that big barn burn down and saw the poor pigs running frantically.

A few years later there was another fire we all saw. We were in the car together coming back from town in the afternoon. It wasn't often we children got to go to town until we were older. Sometimes we would go to a fire sale that one store sometimes held. Our parents felt they might find something we needed or soon would and if they did they had us try the item on for fit. I don't remember what we went for this day. I remember going into the grocery store as our parents were getting our meat from our own special locker they rented. When we came out with a few frozen foods Daddy took them to the car and Mama picked up a few grocery items. Of course we went with her. I so well remember the locker room's special aroma as well as the main grocery area. I remember too the squeaky boards on the floor of the main part of the store and the grocery smell.

As I write I am reminded that the clerks and butchers always wore full white aprons. They were always very friendly and helpful. The wonderful smell of the coffee as Mama ground the coffee beans was unforgettable. Mama didn't let her children drink coffee. With her permission I tasted it and thought it was horrible tasting stuff. That was then.

It rained before we left for town and rained some while we were there. Likely it was because of the rainy weather that Daddy had time to go. We noticed smoke billowing in the distance shortly after we started home so instead of turning where we usually did, Daddy drove straight towards his parent's home as the fire looked like it might be close. Daddy was right. It was just across the road at his brother's place. The barn was burning. It had been struck by lightening just as our cousin's barn a few years earlier. The cattle were out to pasture and no animals were in the barn. Hay in the mow was afire and the barn was burning very quickly. The fire truck was there when we arrived, but the barn couldn't be saved; it burned down.

Incredibly, another afternoon when Daddy was working in the field on his tractor, I noticed a fire that again looked like it could be near our grandparent's home. I ran into the house and told Mama. She took a fast look and agreed and said to run get Daddy. I ran all the way down the lane until I came to the field where Daddy was working. I waved my arms back and forth several times as I began running down a row where he was using the tractor and cultivator. Cultivating requires close watching to get the weeds out without hurting the crop. Daddy was looking downward and didn't see the smoke or me for a few minutes. As I got closer he finally saw me running towards him frantically waving my arms. At that instant he saw the huge billows of smoke, raised the cultivator and came out of the field as fast as he could. He picked me up on the way and we sped towards our house. Mama had already gotten everyone else in the car. Daddy and I got in and away we all went in a hurry. When we were almost there we could see Grandpa and Grandma's big beautiful barn was afire.

Daddy drove fast and was visibly upset. People were just starting to come to help. Daddy's brother was there when we arrived. We could see that at least the hay mow was afire. Fortunately, the cattle were safely out to pasture, but my grandparents two horses were tied with thick ropes to their hay-filled mangers that were now on fire. Clyde and Betty were very gentle huge animals that our grandparents had owned for years. We always pet their velvety noses when we went to the barn. Grandma did the same thing. She loved those horses.

As soon as we arrived Daddy frantically ran to the barn where the horses always were. We were so afraid for the horses. It scared us to see Daddy heading inside the barn as we were afraid for him also. As we children stood with tears running and watching the terrible fire, we saw Daddy's brother run from the barn as fast as he could to his parent's house. In only seconds after getting inside, he came out with a gun and on the run back to the barn. We heard one shot. We all began to cry. Daddy ran from the barn with tears rolling. It may have been partly due to the smoke, but we all knew one gun shot was sad news. He told Mama neither horse could be rescued, but Betty was out of her misery.

Mama and Grandma already knew and they cried together arm in arm. The other horse got loose after its rope burned, but was in the fire somewhere and couldn't be seen. We knew it had to have been burned badly as its mane would have caught fire quickly from the manger fire. Poor Clyde was trapped in the fire and smoke. It was the saddest experience of our lives. We all sobbed together.

We saw a mama cat and her four little kittens run out of the burning barn not long after we arrived. At the time we didn't know they were even in the barn. It was later we learned that they were in the hay mow. Somehow that dedicated mama cat had brought her kittens down the ladder one by one and led them out to safety. She risked her life for them rather than abandoning them to save herself. We were so happy; it seemed a miracle she got them out in time.

After the fire was all over, the skeleton of one big gentle horse lay in the ashes near the center of where a majestic barn once stood and offered safety, shelter, food, and water for the wonderful pair of horses. The other horse's skeleton was near where it was shot. I can't express how terrible that scene was. I have some questions for God someday.

Going to our grandparent's place never felt right again. The whole atmosphere was different. We missed seeing the barn and horses. Grandpa got rid of his cows very soon after the fire and had no desire to build another barn. Grandma seemed to begin to deteriorate in health and was never again the same fun person we once knew. That fire made three barns in a row on a one mile stretch of road that had burned down not many years apart. It was a strange thing and being all relatives made it even more peculiar. All had the same last name on their barns. Two of the fires were caused by lightening, within a few years, yet the barns had stood for many years never having been struck.

There was suspicion that a young boy who was visiting may have lit the fire as he was playing in the barn with the kittens. He would have had to have gotten matches from somewhere, but they were always in a matchbox on the wall at the kitchen entry area near the back door of our grandparent's house. He was questioned but denied starting the fire. No other reason was ever discovered. None of us ever forgot that very tragic day. Just writing about it makes me shudder and brings plenty of tears as the horror of the fire comes so alive again in my mind. It isn't easy to adjust to tragedy. For some it is more difficult than others, but determination to get on with our lives afterward helps in the overcoming process. It seems one has to finally stop focus on self, accept we don't always understand through finite minds what God does and move onward to complete what God has planned for us to accomplish.

Chapter 16

The Irish Couple

My maternal grandparents were neighbors of an elderly brother and sister who came to America during the potato famine in Ireland. The famine began in 1845 and lasted six years. It was caused from an airborne fungus that caused a blight that made the green leaves of the potato plant turn black and killed the plant. Most of the Irish girls married at the age of sixteen and the boys at seventeen to eighteen. Average life expectancy for men was forty years. One fourth of the population was illiterate and very poor and usually had large families. During the famine they had no potatoes to eat or any work in the fields that had produced them. The famine resulted in over a million deaths and another million left the country. Henrietta was born in 1849. I am uncertain when she came to America, but likely she came with her family to escape the potato famine or was born here after their arrival. She and one of her brothers shared a home, as neither she nor he ever married. After her brother died she lived alone. Mother's father and brother did her farming for her on a crop share basis. One day in 1931, the year before I was born, they noticed some corn husks and other debris had blown up in front of the door of her house and decided she hadn't been using it. She was seventy-eight years old so they investigated and found she was very ill with the flu and lying in her bed in a terrible mess and seemed near death. They went to get Grandma to clean her and the bed up before calling the doctor out to see her. Grandma and her only sister were both stricken with polio and both had disabilities as a result. It was very difficult for Grandma to get Henrietta bathed, her hair washed and fixed in a neat bun and in clean clothes and a clean bed. It was determined she may not live through the illness and family living in America were called. She needed help so Grandma kept an eye on Henrietta and tried to nurse her back to health and was present when family arrived. Some of the family who came were hoping for her death and searched for her money; one even checked inside and under the mattress of her bed. Another checked her pocketbook, that today we call a purse, and told Grandma she would take care of it as it contained a lot of money. Likely it was some of her crop money from the farm. Grandma told her it belonged to Henrietta and not to do it. Two of the family went to town to buy her clothes for her funeral. Before the family left, a brother hired a woman to come and stay with Henrietta; probably only until she fully recovered from the influenza. While living alone, my grand parents had aided her when they saw her walking a long distance into Alma for groceries. They often looked in on her and took her into town with them for groceries and anything she needed; Henrietta dressed in long dresses and high cut shoes well above her ankles. She wore binder twine for shoe strings and my grandparents who were very neatly dressed were probably a bit embarrassed to be seen with her but that didn't stop them. The old lady didn't see any reason to spend her money on shoe laces.

They continued helping her after she became too near blind to select her own groceries, but even then, when she was willing they took her along with them for the ride and they picked up her groceries for her. She told them many interesting stories about her life experiences that included relating that, at sometimes, Indians camped on the back portion of their farm property. Her hearing was failing badly. It finally became very difficult to communicate, but that didn't cause my grandparents to stop their aiding her. After Henrietta learned her family wanted her dead and her money, she determined if Grandpa and Grandma continued to care for her she would see that they received some compensation for all they had willingly and generously done for her of their own kindness. She came to really trust my grandparents and expressed they were the ones who really cared for her. She eventually told them it was getting almost impossible for her to take care of herself and explained to them if they would move in with her and take care of her until she died she would give the house and farm to them. She was determined not to leave anything to her greedy relatives. My grandparents knew she needed someone with her and had nobody else looking after her, so they accepted her offer. She was soon completely blind and nearly deaf. I don't know when they moved in, but it is likely that she was in her late eighties as I remember coming to see Grandpa and Grandma when I was around eight to ten years old and Henrietta was still alive and often seated where she was among family and visitors, though in a nearly silent and dark world that must have been a very boring life for her. Sometimes Mama and we children would go see Grandma and Grandpa while Daddy was busy with some work on the farm that he felt needed to be done as soon as time allowed.

Whenever we came to see our grandparents, Mama always talked with Henrietta a little. When we were ready to leave, we each stood next to her to tell her good-bye, because she was made aware we children were visiting with Mama. She was always sitting in her wooden platform rocker, and we had to get right down to her ear to make ourselves heard. I remember how long her ears and earlobes looked. Grandma always fixed Henrietta's hair neatly in a bun and kept her clean and looking neat. I recall well that, as we said our good-byes, Henrietta never failed to tell us to mind (obey) our mother. Sometimes, she mistook Mama for one of us children and told her the same. Mama always clarified who she was and Grandma looked at us and smiled. Because Henrietta was treated so well she grew to really love my grandparents and their family and saw them as her family and best friends. At some point in time, she revealed to my grandparents that she had some gold coins hidden under the floor with access through a floor door. I don't know that she told them the face value of them. My grandparents set such a good example of kindness and caring for others that I am certain we children benefited from what we learned in seeing and understanding their involvement with Henrietta. The experience we had in being in her presence offered its own special value.

Henrietta finally became bedridden. She eventually developed bed sores and Grandma needed Grandpa to help her with laundry every second day as her bedding needed changing more than once daily. My grandparents remained very good to her and tried to keep her well-fed and comfortable. She died four months short of ninety-five. Grandpa and Grandma were at her bedside holding her hand as she lay dying. They took care of the funeral details and she was buried next to her brother.

After she was gone, my grandparents found the gold coins in a velvet bag under the floor. I never knew the face value, but they were eventually passed on to my mother and her brother. Before our parents died my mother gave each of her children two nice gold pieces encased in a container. It was a wonderful gift with some interesting history behind it. I recently learned from a cousin that our Grandma always kept a diary and there was never a thing in any he saw that revealed a negative word her hand ever wrote. That surely reveals one's character. Because of Grandma's well kept diaries, it proved to be a blessing in them winning a legal battle when greedy relatives attempted to get everything Henrietta owned. Both of our mother's parents were wonderful, saintly people and I am proud to be one of their grandchildren.

Our parents did take us places when they were going and it was practical for us to go. We appreciated that though it didn't happen often. I am sure there were times when we were too young to be left alone that Mama had no choice but to take us with her. There was always something new for us children to learn or experience as a result. I remember one time when many people in the neighborhood assembled at the Grange Hall to make mattresses and we children were there to help. I don't recall the reason, but believe it was for aiding the armed forces. Daddy contributed much to his children in ways different from Mama. I recall one beautiful balmy bright moonlit and starry night that on our way home from visiting at our friend's home, Daddy took a detour to a lonely rural road and stopped the car. He sweetly asked us all to be very quiet and listen to the night sounds and intermittent peaceful silence. We heard frogs, crickets, and some sounds we didn't recognize and Daddy explained to us what they were.

He even did his little fun pun by saying," Listen. I hear something. I think it's a noise."

He wanted us to feel the gentle breeze on our faces, and to see the stars and the moon. He pointed out the Big Dipper, the Little Dipper, and the Milky Way and talked about the phases of the moon such as the new moon, full moon, harvest moon, and others. He wanted us to learn about nature and be always aware of its wonder. He told us that, for a test when oysters were removed from the ocean and brought to a state such as Indiana far from the ocean and put in a water tank of appropriate saline water, the oysters would open and close as they always did with the tide that was influenced by the moon and sun. He explained that the tide meant the rise and fall of the ocean's surface water and waters like seas, bays, and rivers that connect it. Daddy elaborated on the tide occurring twice in twenty-four hours and fifty-one minutes, which was called a lunar day. During its rise it is called the flood tide and during its fall the ebb tide. The new or full moon brings an unusually high tide called spring tide. When the moon is at first and third quarter the tide is unusually low and that is what is called neap tide. He always told us interesting things. He even wanted us to smell the clean night air or a field of fresh cut hay that was drying for putting up in the hay mow. Mama had told us that wet hay can mold or heat up enough to cause spontaneous combustion in a mow and that is why it is not put in the mow wet. I remember our parents had us view the majestic northern lights called the aurora borealis and explained briefly what caused them to appear .While some feared them and saw them as eerie, we learned to appreciate their marvelous show of beauty as a cause and effect of God's laws of nature.

Daddy was adept at making a special event even more special. One that comes to mind as I write involves our family attending our paternal annual family reunion. It was often held at Crystal Lake around thirteen miles from our home. It seemed like quite a long journey to us children as it was taken on dusty country roads that sometimes needed scraping to smooth out rough spots. Some places were rough enough that folks called them washboard areas. Those areas made it hard to keep a light weight car on the road. When we began ascending up the long high hill that led to a beautiful view of the small village of Crystal Lake, Daddy asked us to pay close attention because when we crested the hill we could see the huge round building on the lake edge called the pavilion. From our vantage point we couldn't see that the road curved in front of the building. It appeared the road would run directly into it. I well remember the thrill it was to get the first glimpse of the building in the distance. The beautiful building contained a merry-go-round with its special and memorable music and beautiful colors. It had large wavy glassed mirrors on the wall that made us look very warped in appearance from head to toe and was good for plenty of laughs for the whole family and all those who passed by them. We children enjoyed our ride on the merry-go-round. Where the sides of the building were open in places we had a great view of the gorgeous lake as our ride passed by several times. We were thrilled that we were there to experience the magic of the place. Across the street from the pavilion was a small corner store where our parents bought us each a nickel bottle of Nehi soda of the flavor we selected. I remember my first time there that my pick was strawberry, and it was so fizzy that my eyes watered as I took sips. A gulp was too much to handle. Daddy laughed. There were many requests for pardons among us as an unexpected belch slipped out. Swimming was more fun than we could imagine. We didn't have the chance to even splash in a bathtub at home. I remember at one reunion I cut my foot on a broken bottle in the water and went under water to pick it up and bring it out of the lake. Going under water was a new experience for me. The water made my cut smart and I was done swimming for the day. When the potluck we all enjoyed was over, the adult relatives milled around visiting with each other in the afternoon. Many of them, including my parents, sat at the long picnic table sipping lemonade and iced tea. I calmly approached Mama with my smarting and bleeding foot. She examined it, cleaned and dressed it with a bandage and said it would keep the sand out of it. She caringly reminded me that my fair skin had more sun than it needed so I should stay in the shade the rest of the day. She was sorry I had acquired a nasty cut and told me she was proud of me for getting the glass out of the water and throwing it in the trash. Mama invited me to sit beside her and asked if I would like some lemonade that some of the relatives had brought. I was thirsty and I was very thrilled as it contained ice cubes even though I was feeling chilly from the shaded breeze even though Mama wrapped me in a big towel. I have fond memories of our few times at Crystal Lake.

There just wasn't much free time to go to the lake in the summer and that was likely the main reason we seldom went. Once in a great while Daddy took us all to fish in the gravel pit as it was much closer.

Another event that stands out so clearly is Daddy calling all of us children together and telling us he had just heard the war was over. It was an exciting time for the American people. During the war, blackouts were occasionally requested for practice even in rural areas as they would be demanded if America were attacked. It meant no lights on for a given length of time in the evenings. One cold clear night I was out sliding in my boots on the ice near the house and three low flying war bombers came roaring over my head in a deafening sound and very much scared me. I had never heard such a noise as had never been near a plane. I scrambled into the house never considering removing my boots. For an instant, I thought we were being attacked. It was a big relief when Daddy assured me we were not being attacked in America, but agreed it was a most unusual occurrence. He guessed it was likely servicemen from our nation's military that were sons of some neighbors and were flying the planes during a practice mission. We learned he was correct. Looking back I can think of only one place a few miles away from our home where the enemy may have desired to attack, but unlikely. It was the oil refinery at Alma. The next closest towns of much larger size were Saginaw or Lansing and some fifty to sixty miles from our home. Detroit was much larger than either of them and a much greater distance. My imagination allowed for me to believe for an instant that an attack was happening right over my head where we lived in an area with no large towns near us. Children can worry unnecessarily about things they don't understand if their parents don't take time to discuss them. Both of our parents were perceptive and considerate enough to take the time to explain things of our possible concern if it had occurred to them during very busy lives. One concern sometimes is lack of money and children shouldn't have to silently bear that burden. We were aware that Daddy kept abreast of the price of crops and hogs, eggs, and all commodities that related to our income. We knew we had to live frugally and do all we could to make for greater income, but I believe our parents graciously spared us from hearing their private discussions of their concerns about not being able to meet the demand to buy the farm as originally planned. I never felt we would starve to death or not have enough clothes. I feel our parents were grateful that we found means of play that allowed us to live a quite satisfactory life as children. One of my sisters recently reminded me that when going to the woods to play that in the spring we jumped across the stream until we kept trying for wider areas and finally didn't make it across and came out wet. We often visited the stream and watched pollywogs develop into frogs. Sometimes a harmless striped small garter snake would startle us as it slithered away among leaves and ferns and other plants. We generally had little fear of them, except the chance we might unwittingly step on one as were almost always barefooted. Likely, a snake trying to escape our presence was more alarmed than we were. We had paths in the woods where we ran carrying a bent twig in the pretense of it being a bicycle handlebar. Sometimes we spotted a weasel or rabbit scampering away as we came too close for the creature's comfort. One time we spotted a beautiful baby owl on a limb of a tree. There were times we just sat quietly and watched for animals like squirrels or raccoons in the trees or running in the woods. We spent many hours enjoying our woods in many different ways besides picking berries, currents, gooseberries, and spring wild flowers. Another bit of creative fun was using corn silk from fresh sweet corn to put on our dolls for hair. Sometimes we braided it. We made little old wrinkled up faces from old withered potatoes and used the sticky white rubbery content from a milkweed stem to hold hair on them as well as our dolls. If the potato face was to be an old woman we usually make the corn silk into a bun near the top of the head and held it with a toothpick. Eyes pushed-in tiny pebbles from the gravel in the driveway near the road. Sometimes two sprouts from the potato eye would have grown in proper places where they could be removed and the pebble eyes easily implanted. A wee piece of radish peel might be glued on and used for a mouth. If there was not enough nose protruding, a tiny bit of peeling was cut and lifted from a place just beneath where the nose would be and a small lima bean placed horizontally that was held in position with part of a toothpick. The nose appeared as it had nostrils after bringing the loosened peel firmly to the bean .and securing the peel with another part of a toothpick. We made old men's heads, too. Sometimes they had beards and lima bean ears and bushy eyebrows. We made varied faces that taught us patience and ingenuity.

Patience reminds me how patient our grocery man was with us as we tried to decide what we wanted to select for our treat when the grocery wagon stopped near the end of our driveway. Sometimes we selected one called a Guesswhat that contained some little surprise inside. Even our grocery man had his part in contributing to our pleasures of childhood.

Chapter 17

A Big Surprise

With frugal living and much hard work, our parents were doing better financially by 1941 even with added expenses. The economy was improving and crop prices were coming up and that made a difference. Everyone, including my parents I think, was surprised to learn that at the end of June there would be a new addition to the family. It was big news in the neighborhood. Daddy would be forty before the baby was born and Mama thirty-two. Charlene would be five years and four months and starting school and it was four years and nine months since Patricia was born.

The neighbors wanted to have a big shower for the family as they expected the baby clothes were badly worn and they were right. They insisted it be a family affair for the guests as well as all of us. They planned a big potluck meal at noon two weeks from Saturday with each family bringing their own drinks and table service. Folding chairs would be gotten from the church. They wanted it to be fun and easy for everyone. Mama felt we had to come up with some means to entertain all the children. She bought a huge bunch of balloons that we would blow up for a center piece of the long-boarded table held up by two sawhorses that Daddy put together. Daddy came up with the idea of making a whirligig to entertain six children at a time. Four would ride and two push to get it going. He wasn't happy about using some nice planks he was saving, but knew only the ends would be damaged. He made a see-saw on a sawhorse he scrounged up from his father.

A big crowd turned out for the event. After the meal the table was cleared and balloons were passed out to each child. People took their food back to their cars and brought back pastel-colored after-dinner mints in small candy dishes. Along with them, they brought beautifully wrapped gifts they piled on the table. Mama and Daddy were expected to open them as the crowd watched. There was a lovely array of useful gifts, but one took the prize; a blue romper suit for a boy. The person responsible for revealing her humor in this gift was named Dora; she had great fun when that gift was opened. Everyone did. It was a big hit. She told our parents she expected to see blue balloons flying from the mailbox adding she hoped there were some blue ones left in the package. Everyone cheered and clapped. It was a fun day for everyone. My parents were just overjoyed with the wonderful gifts. They told the crowd there was just no way they could offer enough thanks to express how they really felt. Mama said it was a real blessing to have such a group of people as neighbors and Daddy agreed. On June 30, 1940 blue balloons were flying from the mailbox. Even the mailman left a note that said in big letters: Congratulations!

Word traveled fast. People stopped in to see the baby and brought casseroles and wonderful food. Mama told Dora she owed her special thanks; they had a joyful laugh. When Wesley would become eighteen, Daddy would be fifty-eight. Even if he did not choose farming for a career he would be a help to Daddy for a few years. Both Mama and Daddy were thrilled they finally had a son. He was a beautiful little guy who with big brown eyes and very dark hair. I was almost eight when Wesley was born. I loved rocking him and playing with him. After learning to talk, he called Oleta by the name of Eeha, Charlene was Charchie, Patricia was Teesa, and me Teesee. I never have figured out, though Patricia and Phyllis do not have the same sound at all that he started both names with a tee sound. Of course there is no way he could know both names started with the letter P. Mama found it intriguing.

Mama often made pancakes, and if I offered to cut them for him when he was in a highchair, he would immediately say, "No. Mama cutch 'em." Then he tried to cover them with his little dimpled hands. Mama always cut them as soon as she had another pancake or two starting to bake on the griddle. Baby Wesley often liked me to do things with him and I did too, but I never got to cut his pancakes.

I was intrigued with my baby brother. Being old enough, by the time he was born, to really enjoy playing with him and helping take care of him was so much fun for me. It was my nature. I loved baby dolls and nurses kits so I guess it indicated I was a caretaker type. I was a busy type as well. It is interesting how young we are when our innate person becomes overt. A wise parent ought to pay attention to this. It would be a shame to try to squelch an adult child's desire for a certain type of work when they have shown a natural aptitude for it.

Many years later when I became a mother I always taught my children they could become a doctor, nurse, teacher or what ever they desired. When they knew what they wanted to do I encouraged them to focus and stay with it until it was accomplished. I stress the same to my grandchildren. I always regretted that I didn't graduate from nursing when I was really enjoying my education and training in the field. There were many things I enjoyed ranging from nursing to home décor, clothes design for women, hair styling and designing homes. I did get involved in all to some degree over the years of my life. I really wanted a big family and when my fiancé didn't want me working outside the home I quit school, thinking I would never use my nursing.

People are vulnerable to stupidity at that age when a girlfriend or boyfriend is involved. Mama warned us that having an education for backup if ever needed was a good idea. I was wearing rose-colored glasses like so many young people in love do. I found out those glasses have no brains. I quit nursing school at the top of my class and married. In retrospect it was a big mistake. It is much more difficult to go back to finish education later. I could have used mine at times in my life, but when I needed it most the money was not available.

I hope all the youth who read this book heed what I am saying as it is truly for your own good. I know it well as I experienced first hand the consequences of not finishing my dream when I was in the process. Getting your education first is a priority and where your focus needs to be. If your boyfriend or girlfriend leaves you because of your determination to finish education first, then realize that person was truly not the right one for you. Take the silly rose-colored glasses off. With them on you will never see the person correctly. It feels good to the ego to think someone outside the family loves you, but the person you are so gaga about will not be the same person you dreamed in your head. There will be plenty of time when you become more mature to find the right person because you will be more capable of making choices from a more realistic view. You will never have to regret you didn't get your education or not as likely that you married the wrong person. Marrying just because you don't want to be single is almost always a disaster. It doesn't matter how many of your friends are married and it doesn't mean they made the right choice. Likely most didn't.

These photos give credence as to why Phyllis was called " the busy one".

Charlene, Oleta, Wesley, Phyllis, and Patricia

A friend and helper, Mary, Raggie's puppies, Charlene, Phyllis, Oleta, Patricia

Oleta, Phyllis, Charlene and Patricia

Chapter 18

Close Call

Not long after Wesley was born and the other three girls were all in school, Patricia was going to spend the day at her paternal grandparent's home. Patricia was excited because today was harvest day and she could go with Daddy and spend the day with her grandma. She was four and a half years old; still too young for school. Her sisters really enjoyed school and she was lonely. Charlene was a whiz in school and came home and told Patricia all the fun things she did.

Daddy was still not able to pay his father the amount he owed him after the crops were harvested and we still survived living on fifty acres, as they had bought a combine together. Grandpa's navy beans needed to be harvested today as soon as it was dry enough. It took a while to get everything set up for the harvest so the men started around eight o'clock.

Grandma was planning to do laundry. She had opened the door to the cistern where she gathered pails of soft water. The opening was in the floor and she warned Patricia to stay away from it. It was still chilly in the house. Grandma unbuttoned Patricia's coat, but told her to leave it on until the sun warmed up the place a little more. Patricia watched Grandma pull up several pails full of water up with a rope attached. She followed her grandma back and forth from the dining room to the washroom and finally became bored with it and began playing with her top. Grandma was almost done drawing water when she came back for more and didn't see Patricia. She called her name and heard no answer. She looked in the bathroom and the living room and parlor and in both bedrooms. The stairway door was still closed and she was sure she hadn't gone up there as we seldom did. She looked out on the porch. She was nowhere in sight. Grandma noticed Patricia's toy top was still on the floor. A feeling of panic was coming over her. She was not a slim lady, but managed to get down on the floor and drop her head down and call Patricia's name. A weak little voice and whimper responded. Grandma told her to hang on to the boards above her head, meaning the floor joists ,and her uncle would be right over to get her out.

Grandma was frantic and somehow quickly got up and rushed to the phone and called her son's home across the road. Our aunt answered. Grandma told her what happened and to send our uncle over as fast as possible because Patricia had been down in the dark cistern awhile. In moments our aunt was over and leaning down to see if she could see Patricia and told her that her uncle was on his way to get her out and to just keep hanging onto the boards. She could hear little sobs that sounded like they were at the far corner of the cistern but could not see anything. Our uncle worked nights and was home asleep. He came on the dead run wearing only a pair of slippers and pants. He was a stocky man and it was all he could do to get through the opening. He pushed himself down and landed in the cold water. He talked to Patricia and asked her where she was. Her voice would get him in the right direction. He said he would be right there and to hang on to the boards.

She said, "I can't."

To stimulate adrenaline, in a loud voice he said, "Yes you can."

She was just about to let go when he caught her and she put her tired and weak little wet arms around his neck. He told her he would swim over to the opening with her riding piggy back style. She was almost chocking him as he swam.

Her aunt and Grandma pulled her out as soon as he lifted her up to them. Grandma pulled off Patricia's soaked heavy coat and other clothes and immediately wrapped her in a bath towel. Patricia's lip was cut and beginning to swell. She seemed to be breathing normally. It took our uncle a little maneuvering to get himself out of the opening. The first thing he did was close the floor door. He was shivering and said he would be right back. He ran home, dried off, changed into dry clothes and returned. They first thought the wool coat Patricia was wearing may have helped her stay afloat briefly, but it had become very heavy as soon as it was wet. Her hair was all wet and she likely went under with her first splash in the water. Her uncle asked her how many times her head went underwater and she told him two times. He asked how she fell in and she told him she backed up too far when she was trying to keep her top away from the hole.

He and his wife stayed around for a few minutes to make sure both Patricia and her grandma were okay. They noticed Patricia's grandma looked very flushed and was shaking so they asked if she was feeling okay. She said considering the circumstances she was. Grandma wrapped Patricia in a drier towel, carried her to her rocking chair and held her on her lap. Patricia sat shivering and talked very little. Grandma told her she would rinse out her clothes, hang them out to dry, and put her in bed where she could be cozy and take a nap. Patricia nodded. Her uncle told her he wasn't scolding her down in the cistern; he just wanted his loud voice to jolt her enough she would hang on a moment longer. He said he was glad he was there to rescue her and told her she was safe now and would be fine. She thanked him. The couple walked home thinking that accident was a very close call. They knew Patricia's grandma would never get over it if her little granddaughter had drowned.

Patricia soon fell asleep after Grandma put her to bed and tucked her in with a kiss. I doubt her uncle slept soon after hitting the bed. Grandma washed out Patricia's clothes and hung them up to dry. Her little coat was smaller after it dried. Grandma was not in the mood to do her laundry and decided to wait a day, so she set the table and prepared dinner for the men, herself and Patricia. She made an apple pie and fixed a good dinner.

Patricia found dry clothes waiting for her when she awoke and got dressed. Grandma brushed her hair and washed her hands. She looked at the inside of Patricia's lip and it looked bruised. It was thicker than usual, but Grandma felt it would soon be healed. Daddy was surprised to hear what had happened. Before the day was over he planned to go over and thank his brother. By about three o'clock Daddy needed to go home for a tool and took Patricia home with him. It would soon be time for her sisters to be home and he knew she had quite a story to tell them. After rescuing the youngest girl of the family, our uncle remained our hero. Mama and Daddy both let him know how grateful they were for him. Patricia was young, but I have wondered if she was not reared in a home where overcoming was taught if she may have given up. She told us she was almost to the point where she could no longer hang on as she was so cold and her arms so tired. People don't always realize the dynamics of their words or actions.

Chapter 19

More Excitement

On our way home from school we had walked about a half mile on a road with no houses. A hill just beyond blocked the view of four houses near ours. On one side of the road there were elderberry bushes and close to the corner were a few trees along the same side of the road. This particular stretch of road was easily visible by any of the homes on the road and there were no houses near the corner.

A man we had never seen before came by in his car, stopped and offered us a ride home and we declined. He repeated the same thing a few times over the next few months, always coming along when we were at the bottom of the hill and near the elderberry bushes and we always declined. We told our parents, but they never knew when or if it might happen again and couldn't sit there for days. The sheriff's department would not sit for days or weeks out in our rural area in case he appeared. Fortunately, we always were on the side of the road opposite the driver's side of the car. Our parents told us to drop what we were carrying, stay together and run the opposite way he was heading with the car if he ever got out of the car. He had opened his door before and even had one leg out of the car and on the road. He was always dressed in a tall dress hat and black coat or suit and appeared to have a fairly dark complexion. He looked like a very tall thin man and just looking at him gave us the sense he was an evil man. For some reason we didn't really worry about it, but when it happened we always knew it was not a good thing. We could tell he wanted to get us in the car, but we didn't know why. On this day he fooled us as he came from the opposite direction. We spotted him in time and fooled him by running across the road so we would not be on the driver's side of the car. He stopped, opened the passenger side of the door and asked us to get in. We all started running up the hill. We were sure he planned to come down the hill and grab one or all three of us as his door would be right next to us. My

108

parents said he wasn't likely to try it again as he probably knew we had told them because we so quickly ran to the opposite side of the road away from the driver's door and starting running up the hill as soon as he opened the door. That was the last time we ever saw him. He never came back again. We thought if he ever caught a child walking alone on a lonely area of a road he would capture them. I am so thankful we never heard of any such incident and never fell victim to the evil man. It is hard to guess what may have happened if we had not had the presence of mind to quickly cross the road and ruin his plan on the day I consider a close call.

Another close call happened on this same road four houses away from our home. The elderly and very nice Mennonite couple had an ugly acting dog they always kept on a long chain near their back door. The dog always lunged at us if he saw or heard or smelled us when we walked by so we learned to be quiet in hopes he might not know we were there. Sometimes he was asleep; we always hoped he was as we had to walk past the property where the owner's lived. This day he spotted us and made a big lunge at us and broke his chain. He was a big dog. He grabbed Oleta's dress and tore the bottom half right off it. We were all screaming and the owners rushed out and pulled the dog away from us. We were all shaking. They checked to see if any of us were bitten. None of us had been hurt, just very scared. The owners said they would put the dog in the house and immediately go buy a heavier chain for the dog. They said if we wanted they would get their car and give us a ride home. The nice lady said she wanted to apologize to Mama and talk to her about the size dress Oleta wore because she wanted to buy some fabric while she was in town so she could make Oleta a new dress right away. She made Oleta a beautiful dress and said the dog could not break the chain it now had and not to ever worry about again. Oleta tried the dress on for her and it was a perfect fit so everybody was happy.

It seemed we could be minding our own business or playing together when something would suddenly spoil our fun. One nice summer day, we girls went to the woods to pick wild strawberries. On our way to the woods, three children about our ages were waiting in or around their parent's car while they blocked and thinned our sugar beets. It was a customary thing for the Mexican people to do summer work. Many farmers used the people's services for this and other types of jobs as they were very hard workers. The field wasn't far from the woods. We stopped and asked Daddy who was working in another field if we could ask if the Mexican children wanted to go to the woods with us and pick berries. Daddy told us they don't speak English and the parents very little. He said it was a nice idea but just couldn't work as the parents wouldn't understand what we were asking and we would have to get their permission.

We went to the woods and found plenty of berries. We pulled the whole plants out as the ground in the woods was soggy. The plants were small and so were the berries, but plentiful. We made them into bouquets and ate the berries off them. Charlene thought it would be nice to take some to the Mexican children who spent the whole day with little to do while the parents worked and we felt sorry for them. As we reached the car, Charlene reached through the open window of the car to hand her bouquet to the boy maybe a little older than she. He grabbed a crescent wrench and hit her over the head. The blood began to run down her face so we all started running to the house. It was a long run. We all came rushing inside the house and calling for our mama. She instinctively knew something was wrong. We quickly told her what happened. She calmly checked Charlene's head over and saw she had a gash on the top of it. She put a cold cloth on it and cleaned her up. Mama told her to just sit for awhile and the bleeding would soon stop, then Mama said she would put some salve on it. It soon stopped and she added a kiss near her cut head after applying the salve. It was just another kind of medicine. She told Charlene that the parents probably had told them that, if anybody bothered them, to use it as protection. She said the young boy didn't realize she was bringing them a nice gift and he hit her before he thought. I suppose it calmed Charlene a little even if it didn't stop the hurt. It wasn't long before we were sharing berries with her and she was back outside playing with a big goose egg on the top of her head.

We always brought Mama some of what we picked as she very much liked wild strawberries. Once in a great while she made a batch of jam from them. They we so small that it was almost more work than worth the bother. Usually she just ate a few from her bouquet. They always looked pretty in a vase and were available for picking a few every now and then as convenient.

Poor Charlene was hurt again not terribly long after the wrench incident. The Mexican family had finished with the back breaking beet work and were paid and gone. Once again we were going to the woods to play. The leaves were thick on the ground and we were near where Daddy had tapped maple trees and cooked the sap in making maple syrup. Charlene happened to step in an old rusty sap pail that was well concealed on the grassy floor of the woods. Inside it was a nest of yellow jackets. She was barefooted and was stung repeatedly. We all went on the long run to the house as Charlene was really crying. Somehow they didn't sting the rest of us so we other children felt very fortunate. Their sting always seemed more painful than our tame honey bees, and the tame bees hurt plenty. The yellow jackets were not tame bees and likely the reason they were so aggressive.

Daddy seldom was stung by his bees when he collected their honey. They were all around him and several on him. It didn't disturb him. He was pretty well protected with gloves, a veil, and his bird hunting canvas jacket. He said they normally don't sting unless they are hurt from a pinch or being stepped on or harmed in some other way. Mama had one get in her hair once when he had riled them in collecting honey. She was yelling for Daddy to get it out. He came to her rescue and was letting a smile show as he told her to hold still so he could. That time Mama wasn't as calm as usual. I am certain Mama's calm demeanor when we children were hurt was for our benefit.

As usual, she calmly but quickly put a cold wet towel on Charlene's feet and legs and made a soda and water paste hoping the alkaline baking soda would neutralize the formic acid that bees inject in their victims. She gave her a half aspirin and some milk. Mama didn't find any stingers to scrape off so they probably fell off in the run through the woods. She put Charlene on the daybed while she tended to her. Mama watched Charlene for a while and kept applying cool towels to keep swelling down. We always had cold water from our well. Fortunately Charlene didn't show any signs of any unusual allergic reaction to the numerous stings. Mama knew she had gone through a very painful experience. She told her she was sorry she had been stung as she knew it had to hurt very badly. Mama was realistic with her children. She didn't talk down to us. She felt we were able to comprehend more than many parents gave their children credit for knowing. We children felt badly for our sister; we knew she hurt terribly, too.

The next day Charlene was back playing on swollen feet. She was a tough one with lots of grit. Playing on a farm was hazardous. Stubbed toes among us children were about as common as warts on a toad. It was just like another day at the ranch. Mama always cleaned them up with peroxide, then put a little salve and gauze on them and taped the gauze in place. She had a collection of socks so nearly worn out that darning wouldn't pay so she put one on the hurt foot and we could still go without shoes. At the end of the day the dirty sock was thrown out and another one put on for overnight and the coming day. After the second day it was no longer usually necessary. Mama's kisses seemed to have healing power. They, at least, seemed to always make tears stop soon. She kissed lots of toes while we grew up.

Stepping on a rusty nail with dirty feet wasn't exactly rare. We didn't always step in the cleanest dirt in the world. Puncture wounds were dangerous as we never had a tetanus immunization or any other than what we acquired naturally. Lockjaw, as it was often called, was a dreaded illness because death usually came from pure exhaustion from rigid muscles. We were very fortunate that we never were stricken with illnesses following injury with the potential to kill such as blood poisoning. Gangrene was another serious condition we avoided and we never had polio, scarlet fever, or small pox. We did have one kind of measles and chicken pox. I never had mumps, but the other children in the family did. We got very sore throats, ear infections, and chest colds often in the winter. Daddy would rub our chests with Musterole when we had bad coughs. It burned and we hated it. Mama used Vick's Vapor Rub. The red cough syrup she fed us with a spoon was terrible tasting stuff and all I could do to get it down. We must have had good immune systems, but I am sure we kept our guardian angels busy working overtime.

One day Oleta and I were playing in the house and she touched me saying, "You are *it*."

That meant a game of tag began. I was using a ruler and stuck it in my mouth as I planned to spank her with it when I caught her. She ran for the front door to go outside. After getting through the door, she slammed it shut in self defense just as I got to it. The ruler split the roof of my mouth and blood ran out my mouth. As usual, I ran to Mama and she saw the blood. She was in the kitchen and grabbed a clean washcloth and poured cold water on it and put it in my mouth so the bleeding would stop and she could see where I was cut. She had me lay on my side on the daybed and put a pillow under my head. She was her usual calm self. In a moment Mama checked my mouth and found the bleeding had abated. She said she could see quite a long gash on the roof of my mouth. Mama told me I would need to stay just like I was for quite a long time. She brought me a Christmas catalog and told me not to get up until she said I could. Mama checked on me every little while. She told me she would have to feed me soft and bland food for a few days. After an hour she let me get up, but said I needed to play quiet games the rest of the day. Mama fixed me special foods for four days until my mouth healed. She began letting me try firmer foods and soon I was back to eating everything the family ate. Daddy had warned us several times to never run carrying a pencil because he was afraid we could poke out an eye but never said not to run with a ruler in our mouths. Being a good parent isn't easy.

It was early spring and Mama had raked up some debris from the yard. We didn't have much grass except closer to the road. We often played in dirt. After she had a small pile of stuff she wanted to burn, she got the fire going. In a little while it was nearly burned out. Mama returned to the house as I kept an eye on it. I was maybe seven years old, but she trusted me to not get burned and stay until it was out. Suddenly, I heard a pop and felt my arm sting. I looked and blood was running. I ran into the house and told Mama I had been shot. She had her back to me at the moment and her hands full. She asked if I said my eye was shot. I said it was my arm. At that instant she put her items down and turned and saw blood on the floor and dripping from my arm. Once again she calmly went into action. She grabbed a clean white washcloth and pulled it rather tightly over the wound and had me sit down and hold it like she had it. She quickly washed off my legs, arms, and face with a different washcloth, then called the other children and said they needed to get in the car as she needed to take me to the doctor. She grabbed her purse and came and got me and walked me to the car and helped me get in the front seat. She told the others to get in back. Mama told the other children I had been shot. She explained the only logical thing she could imagine was that a shell must have been in a pocket of a pair of Daddy's pants when she washed them. When she shook them to straighten them before hanging them on the clothesline to dry, the shell must have dropped out. She said the shell casing was close enough to the line that it could have happened. Before we got to town, Mama told the other children they would have to wait in the car while she took me into the doctor's office. She said if everybody was good she would buy us an ice cream cone. All of us were very good, including me.

The doctor was able to tend to me almost as soon as I arrived. He had me sit in a chair and he pulled his instrument tray and chair close to me. He sat right across from me with his legs firmly against the outside of mine. I am sure it was done intentionally. Maybe he thought I might kick him. He poured some brownish stuff on a gauze square and painted my arm with it. Next he picked up a small pliers type instrument with one hand, took my hand and wrist and held it rather firmly while he reached in the wound with the instrument with his other hand and began turning the metal out of the hole in my arm. The wound looked liked chewed up fresh meat.

When he was done he poured peroxide on the wound, wiped the area dry around it with a gauze square, put some kind of salve in the wound and wrapped it tightly with many layers of gauze. He covered the gauze with tape and stuck some of it on my skin. He let Mama sit close by as he knew her and felt we both would be fine. He told her the bullet likely penetrated the bone at least some and he would put my arm in a sling for a month. With a smile, he looked at me and said I was very brave and told me I could probably get out of doing dishes for a month. I smiled back and nodded. Mama smiled as he looked at her. She said there would likely be a few other things I couldn't do for awhile as I was left handed. He was surprised. As the doctor told me I was all set, Mama paid him with a check. We went back down the steep steps that led from his upstairs office to the street below near where Mama parked the car. Mama told me she was proud of me as I didn't move or shed a tear while he worked on my arm.

She asked the others how everyone behaved and they said they were all good. Mama was not surprised. As soon as we were ready to go Mama drove straight to the dairy where they had an assortment of flavors of ice cream. We had fun picking out our special flavor. Mine was orange pineapple. Mama had vanilla and we licked ice cream all the way home. It was the most special treat in the world to us all. When Daddy came home for his noon meal he was very surprised to learn what had happened. We never knew for sure how the shell got where it was, but Daddy and Mama were very careful to see it never happened again if they guessed right and it had fallen from Daddy's pocket.

Chapter 20

Four Girls in School

The fall crops were all harvested and our parents still could not pay Grandpa what the original contract read, but things were looking some better. Each year they were hopeful they could get back on track the next year, so they continued to work very hard and lived frugally. Wesley was growing fast. He was a handsome little boy who turned one year old in June. Patricia was in school and loving it just like the rest of us.

We were in the minority with all the Mennonite children as we were taught very different views of religion but we got along all right. The girls didn't wear buttons on their small print cotton dresses that opened down the front. They used snaps to close and open their dresses. They always wore long cotton socks. Their dresses were all much the same style. Mostly they wore long sleeves and their dresses were an a-line style with a fairly wide belt of the same fabric as their dresses and their collars matched as well. They all wore their hair parted in the middle. Until they were around twelve they wore their hair in two braids. After they were confirmed in their church, they wore a black covering that covered their wound up braids allowing only the front of their hair to show. In their church the women wore a-line styled dark coats and a bonnet type covering over their hair. Their dresses were long-sleeved and in dark colors and they wore long black hosiery. The men dressed in black suits but wore no ties. They wore below the knee length black coats. The men sat on one side of the church and the women on the other. No musical instruments were used, just a pitch pipe to tune up for singing. The women wore no makeup and the men wore beards of various lengths and haircuts the same as other people. They were very neat and clean people. All near us were farm people. They used and drove only black plain cars, but didn't use radios in their cars or houses. Their houses had no curtains, only window shades. They did not believe in Santa Clause and saw it as a heathen's belief. They tolerated the Christmas

116

tree in the school at Christmas time. They had no choice since they used a public school and their children participated in the annual program. Some of the songs were not religious songs and some were. When the program was offered some of the Mennonite mothers attended. Families brought in Christmas cookies to pass around at the end of the program. All the students drew names and bought a gift for the person whose name they drew.

My sisters and I spent hours looking at Christmas catalogs where I found all sorts of things I liked. Mainly I wanted a doll that opened and shut its eyes and said "Mama." I didn't like the grown up dolls as much as the baby dolls, but saw them as all beautiful. I liked to look at ones who wore pretty coats with white rabbit fur collars and trim to match at the bottom of their coats and a matching muff on their hands. They were pretty to see, but not the kind I wanted for playing. I wanted doctor or nurses sets every year after I was in school. I always found beautiful dresses and shoes I wished I could have for myself. I dreamed of Santa bringing me a dress that I could twirl in and the skirt would swing wide and beautiful. I nearly drooled over puffy sleeved dresses. There were many temptations in the catalogs for me.

On this Christmas, Mama ordered us dresses for the Christmas program. She found some on sale that looked pretty good to her, but I hated mine. I went to school and stood behind the furnace getting warm. It was the day of the Christmas program and the teacher noticed I didn't seem excited and asked me what was wrong. I told her I hated my new dress but I didn't want to hurt Mama's feeling and didn't tell her I didn't like it. She said that was nice of me and maybe another time I would get one I liked.

A week before our Christmas program a new girl started school. She had beautiful, long, black curls, a pretty face and always dressed beautifully. A half hour before our program was to start her mother came to school with a change of clothes for her. Only in the catalog had I ever seen a dress so beautiful. It was red velvet with a wide white velvet sash that tied in a big bow in the back and the long sash cascading down her dress. It had full puffy sleeves and a big white rabbit fur collar. Her skirt was fuller than any

I ever saw in the catalogs. I just could not stop staring at her. She had on white stockings and beautiful white shiny patent leather shoes with a single strap closing across the top of each shoe. They were gorgeous and my high tops weren't. Her full petticoat made the skirt on her dress stand away from her body and she looked like a princess. Her petticoat had a fancy eyelet-trimmed bottom that showed just a little when she walked or moved. She had a white bow in her hair that was used to tie back her curls in a cluster hanging down her back. She stood out above everybody else. I was simply awestruck. My eyes were fixed on her with barely a blink as I am sure everybody else focused on her too. I have no idea what the Mennonite people thought. I know what I did; I was feeling ultra ugly. She had a peaches and cream complexion and I was getting more freckles every year. My hair had turned to a chestnut brown from dark brown, was curly and pretty, but cut short so it was easy to comb, brush and shampoo. I comforted myself just a little by thinking maybe she had no sisters and I did. We probably had more fun than she. I convinced myself she likely didn't play outdoors but sat around all day looking pretty which sounded very boring to me. I knew my parents could not afford to dress all their girls like she was dressed and it wouldn't be fair to dress only one in beautiful clothes all the time. Mama wouldn't do that. I knew why I wore hand-me-downs and Oleta needed more new things than I did and knew why we wore high tops to school. They were sturdy and supported our ankles.

I talked about her all the way home after school. Mama said it was very possible the girl would much rather be outside playing with us children than having her mother put her in such a fancy dress. She said it probably was the mother's idea rather than the girl's wishes and the little girl may have felt she didn't fit in with the others in school. Mama further elaborated that wealthy people are not always happy people. Many of them concentrate on getting more money or on wanting more and more material things. It seems they are often never satisfied with what they have. They don't always enjoy just being happy with good friends and family and aren't content with a pleasant home and nice furniture, car and clothes. They seem to be searching for something far more than they need. Some of them give no thought to how God instructs people to live where one has true joy in their hearts as they care about others. She added that God has a special purpose for each person and wealthy people sometimes become distracted and don't fulfill their true purpose in life.

As it turned out, the beautiful girl was only in our school a short time and I don't remember she ever played with anyone. Mama explained we are living in tough times because of the depression, but she and our daddy still planned that one day we would live in a much bigger new house that Daddy would build. She said we would have electricity and an inside bathroom and refrigerator and things many houses already had. We wouldn't always be so crowded, but she was glad we still had a house to live in because a lot of people lost theirs when they lost their jobs when businesses closed. She said Daddy still has his work and we are fortunate to live on a farm where we have good food even if it is a lot of hard work. She said sometimes bad things happen to good people and we don't always understand. Our job is to do the best we can in living like God wants us to live. The last thing she said was that overcoming bad things builds character. It helps us have compassion for others much easier than if we were wealthy.

I was glad Mama talked with me about all the things she did as it helped me feel better. I started thinking about all fun things we did like picking Mayflowers, Trilliums , Buttercups, Boys and Girls, and other flowers from the woods and bringing Mama a pretty bouquet. We picked elderberries, wild strawberries, currents, gooseberries, thorn apples, and raw rhubarb and ate them. We made burr baskets. I made a pair of stilts and had fun learning to use them. I really wanted to ask Daddy to put screws in the foot rest, but was afraid he would not want me using the lumber. I used them when he was in the field. Mama knew I made them and did not object. We children played in a barrel where one person was inside and the others rolled it. It was almost as much fun to see the person try to walk after coming out of it as it was to be the rider. I dressed up cats and played with them and gave them rides in my doll buggy. My guess was the girl in the pretty dress had never done any of these fun things. I decided having pretty things was nice, but not the only pleasant thing in life.

When we got up in the morning for school we stood behind the stove to warm up as our bedroom was usually pretty chilly by morning. Daddy added wood before he went to the barn to milk cows but it took awhile to warm our room. To save time we brought our clothes out to warm them and often dressed standing behind the stove while Daddy was out in the barn. We often leaned against the asbestos wall covering as people were not informed then of any health danger of asbestos. A "Happy Hank" program came on the radio on weekday mornings. His purpose was to get children to dress quickly for school with a little ditty in song that he sung.

It went like this: "Get your clothes together in front of the radio. Hurry. Now don't be slow, for this is a dressing contest, let's see who will win, when I blow the whistle you all begin."

It was very effective.

We liked school so much that in the summers we played school in the empty corn crib. We were probably in grades of two through seven when we started doing this. It was a nice school house because it let in light and gave us a roof over our heads to keep the sun from cooking us on hot days, and it often provided a nice breeze. On rainy days we were protected from getting soaked. We left it set up much of the summer. It was our job to clear the corn crib before harvest time in the fall when Daddy made us aware of that fact. Using a few handy empty wood slatted crates for making desks worked well. We turned them upside down using one for a seat. We put straw in burlap bags, folded the open end under and made comfortable seats. Two more crates were stacked for a desk with a piece of wood on top for a smooth desk. Daddy always had such things available. It is interesting that Oleta was always the teacher and she became a teacher later in life. I liked being the student. She had rules we were to obey; if we didn't she wouldn't play. We used last year's tablets and pencils to do our assignments. If we needed to go to the bathroom we were to hold up either one or two fingers depending on need. If we were gone too long, the teacher would wonder what we were doing. She was not so concerned if we had lifted two fingers.

Being a bit of a rascal, I once held up two hands with one finger up on one hand and two up on the other. Miss Teacher gave me a stern look for a moment and tried not to laugh, but was finally unsuccessful. Charlene saw me first, gave me a startled look, dropped her head and tried her best to not laugh aloud. She muffled it pretty well with her hand. I am not sure Patricia saw me as she was the littlest and Miss Teacher had her sit nearest the front. After I came back, Miss Teacher said she had a difficult assignment for me. She probably thought I was bored and she would change that. She was already thinking like a real teacher. She said she would tell me what it was right after recess was over as it was time for our ten minute break. At the session after recess I had picked a very wormy apple and polished it nicely and sat it on her desk. This time she just would not allow herself to smile, but I knew she was about to burst inside.

She held it up briefly and just said, "Thanks for the apple," but did not direct it to me.

I found it in our bed at night. I casually mentioned there was an apple in the bed. I told her I would be glad to share it with her. With a straight face she said she wasn't at all hungry. I told her I decided I wasn't either. She asked me to hand it to her. She placed it at the edge of our mattress against the top bunk railing. Because she was trying to conceal a giggle she pulled the sheet and blanket up over her head for a minute. I was smiling with my back to her. In the morning I got up before she did. I had plans for the apple. I knew where I could find another wormy one, but it was easier and less risky to use the same one. I grabbed it and put it out of sight. She was going to find it in her lunchbox the next time we had school. We were free to play school on this day after we helped Mama for awhile. I suggested we pack our lunches and everyone agreed. When it was time for us to begin school we all brought our lunch boxes. At the 10:30 a.m. recess Miss Teacher made a dash to the privy. I had the apple in my lunchbox and transferred it to hers. I was anxious for our noon recess. When it came we all opened our lunch boxes. Miss teacher saw the apple immediately but said nothing. She got up, walked over to the barnyard and gave it a giant toss. We three girls were roaring in laughter. She didn't crack a hint of a smile. She ignored us and we did her. We talked and whispered among ourselves. She looked like Scrooge while she ate.

One day I came carrying my big rag doll in one arm. The other was behind my back. Miss Teacher said we don't have room in our seats for two people and suggested I take her back. I told her I had an idea of what do with her. She asked what it was. I pulled out a dunce cap I made out of a few sheets of rolled up catalog to make it solid enough to stand up. I used the method of rolling the paper into a cone shape. Next, I folded the slanted bottom edge under in a straight line. It made a perfect dunce cap. I explained that since my rag doll didn't talk, she was dumb and needed to be in the corner wearing a dunce cap. I told her I felt dummies belonged in the corner. Miss teacher in wry wit said for me to put her there as there were three corners left in case they needed to be used. She added it was a dumb idea, but not to take it personally. I laughed and so did she. Moments later she asked where I got the paper for the dunce cap. I told her the most logical place I could think of and where we stack all our outdated catalogs and use them up page by page. She rolled her eyes and held her nose a few seconds. I smiled a big one. She seriously said she asked because the cap was red. I told her I dyed it with some food coloring in water and let it dry. She said she would try to consider it washed. She asked me what I used for a dying vessel. I told her that I used her cereal bowl. She put her finger near her open mouth as though she were gagging. I accidentally slipped out a grin. Charlene had her hand over her mouth, so I knew she was muffling a snicker. Next Miss Teacher said she had an assignment for me. I asked her what it was. She told me after recess was over she expected me to put on a ventriloquist show. I told her it sounded like fun and it was. The dummy had everybody laughing before the show was a quarter of the way along. Miss Teacher told me I got an A for it. The dummy and I were beaming with a smile bigger than life. The dummy's name was Susie. She could never stop smiling. The teacher quickly interrupted my smile and sternly said that I could see that the A stood for awful or awfully well done, it was up to me.

She was good at being a nasty teacher. I told the teacher the show wasn't done yet. She said I could continue. The next thing the dummy said was that the teacher was meaner than a monkey with a broken tail. She added that a broken prehensile tail keeps a monkey from swinging from limb to limb and doing other things monkeys do and makes them grouchy. She said it to the class, not the teacher. She placed her hand near her mouth and leaned forward and whispered it to the students. Charlene and Patricia and I had it hit our funny bones and had to conceal our smiles as much as possible. Patricia didn't do so well. I could hear a giggle and she was right in front of the teacher. Miss Teacher looked stern as a judge. After that Susie looked the teacher's hair over while cocking her head from side to side and looking at the back of her head. This time she spoke directly to the teacher. She said she noticed when she came to teach that her hair was pretty short, but it has grown out a half inch since she started teaching today.

She asked Miss Teacher how many hours a day school would last as her backside was getting numb from sitting on the floor so long. The teacher's response was that the dummy had no feelings as she was stuffed with cotton that started at her head. The dummy tried slamming her arms together but cotton isn't noisy. She hung her head and tried to pout, but her lips wouldn't move because they were only painted on her face in a permanent smile; sometimes that was a disadvantage. Suzie told the students since she was a dummy and was full of cotton that the teacher must be saying she has no senses. Miss Teacher said in her case the words are no sense. The dummy retorted with the fact that she had no cents or dollars.

The teacher told her she was pathetic and to sit in the corner and be quiet. Suzie didn't say another word after that. After I put the Susie back in the corner I was still standing up and raised my hand. She asked me what I wanted to say. I told her I needed some more paper and she asked why. I held up one finger. She told me to sit down and sit in it. I guess I riled her when the dummy said some pretty bad things about her teacher. I explained it wasn't for me, but for Susie as she can't walk and I just saw her put one finger in the air. She asked me which one. I didn't get it and said the one we always use. Miss Teacher said that depends on one's upbringing.

She turned herself so the back of her head briefly faced us. I was sure she heard or saw something naughty done at school last year because when she was turning back around facing us she was trying to get rid of a smile. It took her a moment.

The next time we played school there was a glass of what looked much like cider on her desk. I knew she wouldn't drink it. She asked me what it was and I hedged a little.

She said, "I want the truth and want only the truth and now."

I looked at Charlene and said she had better tell her. Charlene's mouth dropped wide open staring at me.

I whispered, "Winker storm."

Charlene gave me the slightest nod, dropped her head and smiled under a hand over her mouth. Her rounded cheeks gave her away. It was a made-up expression we used when there is a joke or something funny that not everybody present knows. Sometimes we wink at the same time. Instead of a brainstorm, it is a winker storm. My teacher bellowed out that she asked me. She spoke like a sergeant. I gave her a salute. She exhibited a most furious frown, staring at me without blinking. She said to speak up now. It was funnier than ever to me after seeing her reaction. Somehow I managed to maintain my composure by not looking at Charlene. I told her it was urine. She gasped a big one. I still kept myself under control as long as I didn't see or hear Charlene. Her next question was that she wanted to know where it came from. I told her I just happened to have a glass in my hand when a cow lifted its tail. She looked at me in a long stare. I waited it out staring back at her without a blink or hint of a grin. She said once again she was asking for the truth. I soberly admitted I hadn't told the truth. She said it was high time I did and if I was smart I would do so now.

I told her I went to the privy with an empty glass and came out with a full one. Miss Teacher gasped once again and got up from her chair, walked out of the corn crib school house and over to the barnyard and tossed the contents. The wind caught it and she found out what a back splash was. She rinsed out the glass, washed off an arm and her face and came back with them wet. While she was gone we three girls saw it all and had a wonderful laugh. Miss Teacher marched, still resembling a sergeant, back to my desk and plunked the glass down. She said to take it to the house now and put it in the dishpan under the sink and be back in thirty seconds. I looked at her and decided to do it. I was having too much fun to have her quit teaching.

Upon returning, the teacher said she had a special assignment for me. I was anxious to hear what it was. She told me she wanted to write down why the chicken *didn't* cross the road. I told I knew of three that didn't. She said she wanted me to tell her right at the moment. I said the first one was hit by a car and became gutless. The other students roared. The teacher hushed them. I said the second one was colorblind and couldn't tell the grass was greener across the road. I added that the third one was just a big chicken.

Charlene lost it that time; the teacher grinned at her. I sat waiting for Miss Teacher's response. I thought maybe she would say I would get a real A this time, and it meant well done. After a brief moment she said that it was a two-part question. She asked me if I was ready to give her a quick answer. I explained that until I heard the question I couldn't answer this one. She gave me an icy stare. She may have been stalling in trying to come up with a question. I was enjoying it and was very curious what it would be.

Suddenly she said she wanted me to answer why the chicken *did* cross the road. She was snapping her fingers while saying, "Quick, quick, quick."

I immediately said the first one did because it had the guts to do it, the second one wasn't colorblind and the third foul just wasn't a chicken. The other students laughed out of control. With a poorly controlled grin the teacher said we could all be excused for ten minutes. She ran over to the house. I think she was telling Mama how school was going. I could hear them both laughing, but didn't want to let them know it.

Besides, I was busy. I saw a big, mean, prickly thistle just behind the privy; things grew best there. I grabbed the shovel and cut a chunk off the monster and cautiously picked it up and ran back and carefully placed it inside Miss Teacher's chair pad. Before we came back inside the schoolhouse I told the two girls. We all came back on time and sat at our desks. Our teacher didn't sit. Charlene gave me a quick glance as I did her. Miss Teacher asked us to pay close attention as she had a few words to say. We did pay very careful attention to her. They were words of a sermon regarding not being late in getting our assignments done and to be considerate of others. We three girls were enjoying her talk. The teacher had no idea why we were attentive at the moment. She asked if we understood. Amazingly, in unison we all responded by telling her that we understand very well.

She stared at me a moment and asked what was up as she smelled a rat. I responded by telling her nothing was yet, but would be when it came down. She looked above her head, shrugged and walked to her chair. All eyes were on her as she walked to her chair to sit down. She didn't stay a half second on her chair seat.

She came off it like a bullet and yelled "Ouch!" so loud it echoed off the barn.

Immediately she began rubbing the posterior portion of the body that touches the seat first as one sits. We three girls knew we didn't dare let out a squeak right at the moment. I used my hand to block the view from Charlene or I would burst aloud uncontrollably. I could see Patricia's hand over her mouth and a rounded cheek above. I felt I would burst holding in my laughter.

Mama was out taking some clothes off the line and thought she ought to investigate what happened. She walked over, stepped up and asked if everything was okay.

Miss Teacher, still rubbing her posterior, said "Not exactly." She asked Mama if there were thistles in straw.

Mama said "Not under normal circumstances."

She looked at me and walked away laughing. We all lost our composure right then, but were quickly hushed. The teacher sternly called me up to the front and told me to take the thistle out. She stood very close to see if it was a fresh one. It was very fresh.

After school was out for the day and it was bedtime, I noticed a bit of a lump in my pillow. With Oleta and me sharing the same bed, I thought about switching pillows. I decided it would be more fun to just get rid of the thistle I found inside my pillow case and let her wonder why I wasn't reacting. I removed it before she got into bed while she was making a privy run. When she came back she was most surprised to see me using my pillow. I even scrunched it up under my head, then the side of my face. I turned my back to her and had a grin that would make a Cheshire cat envious. Neither of us mentioned the thistle. That kind of silence was so much fun.

The next time we played school she was putting me to the test and I must have been exasperating her. She sent me running on errands for things she needed from the house. I did what she asked. After I got back she asked me if I would get her an aspirin. I told her she must be punishing me as I just left the house thirty seconds ago. She told me she was the teacher and to do as I was told. She said the first time she *asked* me and now she was *telling* me to get her an aspirin for her splitting headache.

I thought she was trying to get rid of me, but I played dumb. I like fighting fire with fire as it works so well. I told her I knew right where there was one close by. She looked surprised that one would be near. She asked me where it was. I responded by telling her I saw Daddy take one from his overall pocket and accidentally drop it on the ground of the barnyard where the animals came for drinks from the water tank I explained that it happened just as he was going to get a drink of fresh water from the faucet to rinse it down. We students all heard a gasp followed by a long sigh from my teacher. She dropped her head on her desk for a good minute. I thought I saw her shoulders jiggle a little. Charlene and I were giggling, but trying to be quiet. It was not easy. Poor Patricia was sitting too near the teacher to have the fun we were.

When the teacher lifted her head she told me not to bother that she needed at least two now and she preferred getting her own where she could get two from the same place at the same time. I told her I understood. Charlene almost blew it with laughter when she heard my response. Of course she didn't really need any as we seldom used them and never more than one.

She was waiting to hear what would come out of my mouth. My story was just made up as hers. I was waiting for her response as we were playing our rolls. It was so much fun. That is how part of our playing school went. If we never learned much else, we did learn wit. When Oleta told Mama some of what went on, she laughed till the tears ran. Mama always said I knew how to have fun even if it was borderline dangerous or naughty.

Charlene liked it when I made up stories and told them; she preferred the spooky kind. We had made a tunnel in the hay that was in the mow. Our tunnel was long enough that we all could crawl in it at one time. It had just enough room at the dark end for us to sit. We found it a good place for spooky stories. They were always most thrilling when told in the dark.

I told many, but one I made up always had a part of it that said, "I'm coming up the first step, Mary." Then I paused a few seconds and repeated, "I am coming up the second step, Mary."

I repeated that a few times as there were ten steps. Poor Mary had no place to run or hide as the mean ogre was after her. She tried, but he always caught her. I would tell it a little different each time regarding where she tried to hide. I never changed the end where she always was caught by the ogre.

At the end of my story when I said, "Gotcha!" nobody knew ahead of time who I was calling Mary.

Who I picked to grab was always a surprise and they always jumped nearly out of their skin. We didn't have much for toys, but we knew how to make our own fun. We made the most from a less than desirable situation, but I don't think we ever really thought of our lifestyle as undesirable. As we became adults and lived a different style of life we realized that we had survived pretty well with what we had. That includes our parents as well as us children. I doubt that many children had any more fun than we did. I doubt, too, that when we were a little older that many worked harder than we did.

I have no regrets. We all needed to pitch in a pull together to overcome adversities. I am certain our hair, bodies and clothes became dirty quickly with the kinds of things we did. It meant much work for Mama, but she so gracefully tolerated our shenanigans and varied forms of play.

Chapter 21

Mama Goes Back to Teaching

Wesley was three years old and we were still living in the same tiny house as Daddy just couldn't seem to get enough money ahead to get back on his payment plan to his parents. Mama went back to teaching school to help bring in more money. It also meant she had to take college courses the rest of her teaching years. It was an extra burden on top of teaching, but she did what was needed and always did it well. I don't know how she found the time and energy to study or do her class assignments as it was done at night out of necessity. A hired girl looked after Wesley for one school year. The next year Mama taught near her parent's home and Wesley stayed with them on weekdays as Daddy was too busy to tend to him.

She taught for twenty-four years after she went back to teaching. I am sure she did a very good job and was fair and was not one who gave good grades unless they were earned. Knowing her code of ethics well, there is no doubt she was there to teach and wanted her pupils to learn. She refused to teach where her children were in her school or classroom. When she brought work home like correcting papers of student assignments, the grades she gave were kept private from her children as it was with report cards. She was a lady of high morals all her life.

We children helped more with farm chores and household duties. Everyone old enough pulled together to make things better. We understood and saw it as being a need for family participation. Mama needed help with getting produce picked and prepared for canning as she only had Saturdays after school started. That was the day the house was more thoroughly cleaned and laundry done, so canning on that day required much help from her children. Daddy sometimes had us pull mustard weeds out of the fields. It was hard work, but we didn't complain although our backs did.

One year we three older children hoed a field of beets in hopes of getting a bicycle that we were promised. Hoeing meant hand-pulling the weeds as well as using the hoe when the weeds were too close to the beets. It was slow going and took us several days of hard work. Unfortunately, that year our beets developed a fungus disease called black rot and the entire crop was lost so there was no money for a bike. Daddy felt sorry and bought us soda pop as some compensation.

I liked being outside. The jobs I did helping Daddy were sometimes very hard and sometimes dangerous. I remember while pitching straw, that I ran the pitch fork tine through my bare foot between my big and second toe, pulled it out and kept working. Daddy poured turpentine on it when we were done and back at the house. Another time while Daddy was combining wheat I was running the bagger and a lock of my shoulder-length red hair caught in a spinning pulley. I had no choice but to give my head a quick jerk to pull the hair out of my head and free myself. It hurt, but I only had seconds to do it. I never told my parents. I didn't want Daddy to feel guilty he had never thought to warn me about the pulley. My hair that was left on the pulley wound tight and was black with grease so Daddy would never know what it was. We just kept going with the job when conditions were right for harvest. It kept me too busy to think much about it, but I checked for a bald area when at the house. It was where I could keep it covered until it grew back. That experience taught me to be very cautious around a turning pulley.

I was getting to the age where I very much disliked my freckles and for my twelfth birthday, I wanted only one small item—Stillman's freckle cream which I saw in an ad in *The Farmer's Wife* monthly magazine. I still have the magazine with the ad in it today. It is so interesting to look at advertisements and articles in this old magazine. The one I am viewing is dated, August 1925. One full-page article addresses rural school problems. One problem was where the teacher would room and board for the school year. Another is the teacher having to take a cold-packed lunch, while another is having to drive in bad weather. It was not the teacher complaining, but a concern of those on the school board and those who had children in school. Another interesting article of nearly a full page asks, "Are your children healthy?" and shows concern about feeding and caring for children. There are also wonderful stories for mothers to read to their children. There is no foul language in the magazine. Dignified dress patterns are offered for purchase. It seems such a self-sufficient and innocent era compared to what today's magazines depict. I don't think I have seen it since I got it for my birthday. It cost a quarter. The instructions for its use were to stay out of the sun, but that was impossible for me. I lived with freckles the rest of my life and I am certain Mama knew that my using the cream was futile. In her wisdom she deemed that the quarter would be well spent and I would better come to accept that redheads have freckles. I feel it did help some. I told myself that people are each unique in many ways and in appearance. Some have double dimples as an attractive feature. Others may have a well shaped face, beautiful eyes, nicely contoured nose, beautiful hair and any number of features that appeal to the eyes of the beholder. They vary as much as physical features. In the animal kingdom we see stripes, spots, solid black, brown, white and a great variety. Just as at a dog show there are all sorts of shapes, sizes, and colors.

People have their own preferences for what is beauty; it makes life interesting. I remember Mama telling me as I aged my freckles would become less visible. What she didn't say was that was because age spots called liver spots would overshadow them. As I aged I always kidded her about it. Her sense of humor approved. As I became a young adult I babysat and earned money for makeup to cover the things. I guess they were not as unsightly as I had at times imagined or the makeup did its job. I finally realized I only disliked them on myself, not others.

A few years after I married and had children, I modeled for various hair design artists who were in national competition at hair shows. My hair turned red before I was through elementary school. Being naturally curly and naturally red made me be sought out by artists. We placed well at the shows and it was a fun experience. I modeled in high styling where models wore long dresses. That was a good thing a farm girl as I was never taught to walk like a model. As each model walked the runway the song that represented the state of the artist was played as it created a pleasant atmosphere. The artist agreed to shampoo, style, and cut my hair for free for a year each time we placed and we always did. Winning at the national level was quite an honor for the artist and a nice reward for me. I did it for a few years. After that my kids and household duties kept me too busy.

Many years later I modeled for another artist in Traverse City who did local hair shows to advertise his business. We were living in the area when I stopped by to see about a haircut and he asked me to model. He wanted to present a one model show where he would shampoo, cut, and style my hair in front of an audience. I was grateful he asked me to model for him as it had monetary value for me. However, he glued long lashes over mine and I was allergic to the glue; so I was modeling with blood shot eyes and a runny nose with no time to do anything about it. The audience was made aware of the problem and applauded me for going ahead with the show and later told me it was barely obvious. Life is full of surprises. How we handle them can make a difference in our lives.

Chapter 22

The Economy

World War II broke out in 1941. The economy in America began to change not long after. Many women went to work in factories to replace the men who went to fight the war. Some of them went to war too. After the war ended many women continued to work outside the home and the economy was on the upswing.

I finally got the ice skates I had wanted for so long for Christmas. We three older sisters all got them, so now we could go skating together on the big pond that froze every year on the farm just east of us. I just knew I could skate right away and I did. It was so much fun. After we had our chores done, we spent hours on the frozen pond in the winter days when we were not in school; not even the worst weather daunted us.

Daddy went back to cutting more wood because he felt by the time the lumber was dry he might be able to build our long dreamed of new house. Our parents never gave up on that intention and with the children getting older it was a badly needed change.

While we were still in elementary school all the rural schools were asked to have the children go into areas of milkweeds and pick the pods for making parachutes which America needed for fighting in the war. We non-Mennonites, at least, were proud to collect milkweed pods for making parachutes for our service men. Our school, being the largest rural school in the county, collected many gunny sacks full. The Mennonite students helped, also even though they were conscientious objectors in fighting in the war and killing people.

June 6, 1944 was D-Day, the day of invasion on fifty miles of the Normandy coast. There were 160,000 troops amassed to fight the Germans and liberate France. It was the long awaited invasion, the biggest gamble, and the most brilliantly disguised in a war of constant Allied amphibious landings. The invasion was planned for June 5, 1944, but there was a terrific storm in the English Channel. The weather proved to be not much better on the next day when the invasion began. Even a 30,000 ton battleship, the Nevada, rocked in the water like a bathtub and the men were all sick and vomiting. So many rounds of ammunition were fired that it took three days for the guns to cool off. The noise was deafening. The recoil from a five-gun salvo of the fourteen-inch guns moved the battle ship Nevada back eighteen feet in the water. Sitting down or leaning against the bulkhead was never done as the concussion would break one's back. Of the 30,000 young men who died in the fierce battle, 21,000 were Americans. Many paratroopers dropped in the water. Some were shot on the way down, or broke their legs when landing, and some drowned in shallow water in flooded fields or in the sea because they were loaded down with two hundred pounds of gear.

Hitler had an intuition that the invasion would be in Normandy, but he kept his best divisions in the Pas de Calais opposite England's Kentish coast. Normandy was chosen for our allies as it had a sloping beach rather than the cliffs of Calais. Hitler's commander in Normandy, Erwin Rommel, an enemy of genius in North Africa and the conquest of France in 1940 suspected Calais. He felt the Germans must repulse the Allies at water's edge or lose the war. The results are history. V-E Day (Victory in Europe) soon followed as Germany surrendered on May 7, 1945. I remember right where I was when I first heard the news about the surrender of Germany via radio. I was so happy. It was the biggest news in America. Everyone seemed to be talking about it, including Daddy. I would turn thirteen on July 24, 1945. While walking down a street in Ithaca, I recall the thrill I felt with it being V-E Day. There was going to be a celebration parade in town.

In America in 1944 a bottle of Coca-Cola cost a nickel, the St. Louis Cardinals were on their way to a third consecutive World Series, *Oklahoma* was still playing on Broadway where one could buy a ticket to see *Carmen Jones* for three dollars, and at Harvard , scientists were building the first general-purpose, digital computer. A public school teacher earned an average of seventeen hundred and thirty dollars per year.

I never really knew how the Mennonites felt about helping provide the milkweeds for war purposes; maybe they felt since they lived in America it was the thing to do. I never discussed their religious beliefs much with them. Though I once went to their church, I never got over the strangeness of having no organ or piano to accompany their singing. It was an interesting experience, but one I never really understood. It just felt strange to me that no musical instruments were used in their service.

During the depression years, animal feed and mash for feeding chickens came in cotton printed feed bags. When empty they were washed and used to make clothing. Mama used them to make dresses for us and sometimes she made herself an apron. Most of them were attractive designs and it exemplified the waste not, want not attitude of the post depression era.

One early spring, about six months after Patricia was born, we had an incubator in our parent's bedroom closet; a small closet with few clothes. There was room for it near one wall as Patricia no longer slept in the bassinet in our parent's bedroom but slept in our girl's bedroom in the crib we all had used. The bassinet was folded down and covered for storage at our grandparent's big house. There would be other springs that baby chicks would hatch from the incubator in the same place. Our parents needed more chickens so hatching baby chicks was a good idea and less costly than buying pullets. We had finally gotten electricity which provided us with light bulbs to heat the incubator. It was wonderful to have electric lights in the house and not have to pump water by hand, but we still had no running water in the house. Having an electric toaster was great. We children took great advantage of that.

We had success with hatching little chicks that soon became pullets, and then grew into egg laying hens. It wasn't long before we had more eggs to sell for income. Over the years there would occasionally be a rooster from the hatches, but they usually lost their heads after maturity and did the rooster dance right after for a moment. We kids saw some unpleasant things sometimes, but our parents explained it was not as bad as it looked. Our parents told us it was so fast the birds barely felt it. They told us with such thin necks that the spinal cord is only a short distance inside their necks. They explained the roosters don't even feel it more than a split second since once the spinal cord was severed it has no feeling. Daddy used a block of wood and an axe. He was very careful to do the job correctly and bring instant death. It was very strange to see a rooster hopping around maybe five seconds with its head missing but that is just what happens in that case. The roosters provided food for our family.

During the war in the first half of the 1940s, sugar, coffee, gasoline, and tires were rationed. Each family had a certain amount of coupons to use within a given period of time. If a family ran out they could not buy again until new ones were issued. After the war ended in 1945, surplus foods were given to schools and other institutions. We had free honey butter, peanut butter, plain butter, and a few other foods. The free butter was great for our raw potatoes that we baked at school. It all was a marvelous help to families. After the fall crops were harvested, Daddy finally had enough crop money to pay his parents the full yearly amount he owed. It was a blessed relief for my parents as we could now live from one hundred acres instead of fifty. It took almost fourteen years for that to happen.

Daddy spent five years cutting trees, preparing and drying the lumber and finally building the long-planned big two story house by himself. We so looked forward to the day we could move in. By 1947 Daddy had everything done but the flooring in the living room and dining room. In a few days we planned to move in our big new house. The open stairway was finished in an attractive wood grain with varnish that made it shine, enhanced the grain and protected the wood. The plastering job was done by a professional who did it beautifully; as smooth as an eggshell. The woodwork was in cherry wood and beautifully finished. We had a lovely house. It was almost impossible for us to envision what it really would be like to live in a house with lots of space and running water. Having a refrigerator meant we could have ice cubes; the first time in our lives that we children ever had that luxury in our home. We could barely imagine having a bath tub and shower. It would be such a blessing to be able to shampoo and rinse our hair with ease. An inside flush toilet seemed like only a dream. A bathroom sink where we could brush our teeth and rinse down the sink was going to be a pleasant experience. Having modern laundry appliances was a huge advantage that we were already enjoying and with a sewer we never had to worry about carrying out water again.

The clothes dryer cut ironing time down and improved fabrics were helping. Better fabrics were available to us as we had more money for buying them. An electric stove where the temperature could be regulated made us all excited about cooking and baking. Three of us were already in high school. Our new house had a big kitchen and Mama wouldn't have to swelter in a tiny kitchen working over a wood heated cook stove anymore. We four girls were greatly looking forward to only sharing a bedroom with one other person. It would be so good especially in the warm months not to feel crowded. With four of us stacked in twin beds and Wesley in a crib, we had only a little space to walk in the middle of the room. There were so many things that would feel like luxury to us that we were counting the days before it became reality. We were about to experience a great change in our lifestyle. I would turn fifteen this year and was overjoyed that I could spend part of my high school years walking out the door of an attractive house. I am not sure I ever told my father how much I appreciated him building it, but I hope I did.

Chapter 23

Johnny's Tragedy

When we children were old enough to stay home alone, my parents were invited to take a trip to the state of Washington. Their friends wanted them to join in their journey to visit one of their older children who lived there. My parents had been somewhat acquainted with the son the parents desired to visit.

Our parents had never taken a vacation since they married. There was about a week's lull before harvesting was necessary and it was a good time to go. We told our parents we were comfortable with them going. Our grandparents lived close by and we had neighbors across the road. There would be no need to use the heating stove and we knew how to cook things from the garden and other foods. We thought it would be a fun adventure for us to stay home on our own for a few days. Wesley would stay with Mama's parents as he enjoyed being there and they enjoyed him. We girls were left with many instructions of do's and don'ts.

One big don't was to never light a match near the gasoline barrel. We girls viewed our first dead person from such an incident. It was a boy in about the third grade who went to our rural school, but was younger than the three of us. He was immediately engulfed with flames from the explosion that incurred. After his death all the pupils were let out of school to see him at a casket viewing. It was a sad day and most of us were blinking back tears. It seemed more like a dream to me than reality. He had chewed on his bottom lip from so much pain that he didn't look at all like he did when alive and healthy. It was a shock to us. I am sure it taught everyone a lesson they never forgot. He was burned so badly that he developed an infection that killed him. At that time there were no antibiotics and a burn over one third of the body was usually fatal and his burns covered more than that. He was transported to the university hospital in Ann Arbor which was a long journey from his home. They soaked his burns in oil baths and treated

him for many days before he died. He suffered terribly. I remember well
the day the accident happened. His older and very sweet sister who was no
longer in school met us in front of their house and along the road as we
were walking home from our rural school and told us he had been badly
burned and taken to the hospital by ambulance. We felt badly about the
awful accident and missed the little guy in school.

While our parents were on their trip, Grandpa and Grandma would
check on us as we had no phone, but in an emergency we were told to use
the neighbor's phone as they lived across the road. Grandpa agreed to do
the milking and would be over twice a day. We children got along very well
caring for ourselves and gathering, cleaning, and crating eggs for sale. They
were picked up by a buyer on a regular basis. Once in a while an egg would
be accidentally broken while still in the chicken coop, sometimes by a human. We didn't think it should be saved for us to eat. Charlene and I found
they made great mud pies; they were nice and shiny after they sun-baked
behind the chicken coop.

One day, when our parents were on their journey with their friends,
we were outside playing and discovered our beloved big yellow tom cat
pulling himself up our driveway. His back legs had been cut off. As we
stood in unbelief he was dragging himself toward the barn. I remember
well his big yellowish green eyes looking up at us. He struggled in pain so
we didn't touch him, but talked to him a little. We knew something had to
be done immediately. We didn't want the suffering animal to crawl where
he couldn't be seen and maybe starve to death or die after many more hours
of agony. We had to act fast. Oleta and I decided to call a neighbor we liked
and told him what happened and to please come quickly to shoot our poor
cat and put him out of his misery. We were all in tears as he came very
quickly. Our poor suffering cat had managed to pull himself inside a big
tile under the barn and crawled on through it to the ground. The neighbor
could see it, but didn't know for how long. He said we did the right thing
and asked us to quickly go in our house. By then we were all crying. Our
neighbor man was able to shoot the cat. He came to the door and told us
the cat never felt it and said it was the only thing to do for it. He told us if

we needed anything to let him know. He was very empathic and told us he was so sorry about our cat. The neighbor across the road was cutting hay. We decided the cat was over in the field hunting for field mice when the mower cut off its legs as it crouched in fear of the tractor, not the extended mower blade. We never knew how far out in the field the cat was, but we knew he somehow managed to pull himself from the field and across the graveled road and through a lot of dirt of our long driveway to the barn. It had to be horribly painful.

Our parents were horrified upon learning what our wonderful Johnny cat had suffered while they were gone. They agreed we were very brave in deciding the poor animal needed to be put out of its misery and told us they were proud of us. Everything else went well and they commended us for doing a good job and being responsible kids. They said they knew we would be or would never have gone on their trip. We were pretty proud of ourselves.

In the winter months our parents played cards with two or three other couples every other Saturday night. They all took turns entertaining. When it was our turn, Daddy made various flavors of homemade brick ice cream. Ice was available from the horse tank and buckets if desired. We had most ingredients he used in the ice cream available with little cost. He made ice cream that exceeded delicious and was the treat of treats, even better than Daddy's occasional homemade candy.

Other than the six day trip, it was pretty much the only fun entertainment my parents had except attending one or both annual family reunions and occasional visits to or from relatives and one family of four. We were happy they had something fun to do that was affordable. They included us when practical.

Oleta loved to hear radio stories. On Saturday nights, a spooky story came on a radio program that was called *Intersanctum*. Daddy was not home to listen to his favorite news casts so we listened to the scary story while our parents were gone not far away for a few hours of fun and fellowship with some good friends. Daddy used coal on those nights so we didn't have to open the heating stove door.

One night we found a large box my parents had gotten with something delivered in it. We brought it in the house from the granary and all climbed in it and listened to the spooky tale. Somehow it offered us comfort with us all so close together; it made no sense, but was fun. Nobody ever locked their doors. The neighborhood was deemed safe. Our parents had a surprise like bubble gum for us when they left for a few hours for a little fun with their friends. When children don't often get surprise treats, it is amazing just how wonderful a wad of bubble gum is. Sometimes it became pretty stale after being parked on our bed post, but it was hard to give up so we chewed it the next day. We didn't get to hear stories on the radio very often. Oleta sometimes found one to listen to in the daytime when she wasn't in school. Mama may have kept an ear tuned in when she could. The scary ones usually were told at night and we had to go to bed by 8:00 p.m. Daddy listened to his favorite stations in the evening and at night and occupied the use of the radio.

Daddy never seemed afraid of anything except mushrooms. I remember as a young child seeing him and Grandpa trying to break a young horse while the horse reared up on its hind legs and was totally wild. Daddy seemed to have no fear, but I thought he could have been killed. It was so wild they could never train it and was sold for dog meat. Its mother was the horse that bit Oleta. I remember Daddy telling when he and a friend had gone deer hunting in a northern forest near Atlanta, Michigan. He was returning to camp after dark and an animal was stalking him. When he stopped so did the animal. He tried it several times, but it stayed slightly behind him and just to one side. Daddy said he guessed it was probably a lynx, but never got to see it. He said it sort of raised the hair on the back of his neck, but mainly he was just curious to know what it was.

In the fall Daddy always found mushrooms; sometimes he gathered enough for two big meals. He knew where they were but would not tell anyone. A cousin tried to find out but he would not tell and it became sort of a joke between them. Daddy knew how to have fun. He often revealed his sense of humor and people enjoyed his company. He also knew things many people didn't because he made a point of learning. Daddy had studied about all the mushrooms growing in Gratiot County. He knew some were edible, but some were very poisonous and led to a quick death by affecting the blood. Before he would allow any of his family a bite, he and Mama cleaned them thoroughly and rinsed them in salt water to get rid of any bugs they might contain. After that was done, Daddy looked every one over carefully though he had examined them as he picked them. He was very cautious with mushrooms because the edible and poisonous ones looked very similar. If any were suspicious to him, he fried pieces of them and fed them to his hunting dog. He knew it would become ill soon after ingestion if it were not safe to eat. If the dog remained happy and healthy he approved of them for his family. He never had a dog die from them. Mama rolled each one in a light coat of flour and fried them in lard from bacon. We thoroughly enjoyed eating them. I always thought they were better than any meat.

We knew Daddy liked his hunting companion very much and kidded him about being so highly favored over his dog. He enjoyed our humor. Daddy had fun with his children telling us about Jackalopes and Killdibbles and other made-up creatures. He would sometimes repeat the poem of Timothy T. Twitters. It was a real tongue twister and fun to hear him repeat.

He would sometimes suddenly say, "Listen I hear something. I think it is a noise."

His father had some of that same humor in him. When we were very young and fell down, he would say, "Come here and I'll pick you up."

Daddy enjoyed asking us children the question of if a tree falls in a woods and nobody hears it, does it make a noise? We would say it did because the animals could hear it. He would ask what if no animals were in the woods to hear it? We answered that it still made a noise because trees always do if they are heard or not. I remember saying if a radio is on, even if I don't hear it, the radio is still making noise and he always responded with a smile. Sometimes he would mention that using the gray matter between our ears was not a bad idea.

Daddy was very capable of getting on a rampage sometimes. Usually it was triggered when he felt the need to repair something that needed it as soon as possible and couldn't find the tool required. He would accuse us children of taking it. We knew we hadn't without putting it back as we learned pretty young that it was a big no-no not to leave it where we found it. It upset us to search for a tool that was missing as it was always found where Daddy left it.

Daddy did not want us to make noise so that he couldn't hear the fights when they were broadcast when boxers like Joe Lewis and Max Baer fought. Gabriel Heater and Walter Winchell were his favorite nightly newscasters. He found Walter Winchell of great intrigue as he knew his background. He found it interesting that Mr. Winchell quit school after the sixth grade and was in vaudeville for several years. I well remember his unique method of news casting. Before he told each story there was a sound of a telegraph key in rapid-fire staccato style that indicated an urgent message to follow. Even when very young it attracted my attention. We were to be quiet while he listened to the radio. Some newscasts occurred after we were in bed since we always went to bed early. Sometimes when it was still daylight outside it was hard to do when we could hear the next door neighbors still playing outside and having fun. With four of us girls in one room and two in a bed, we would get to laughing and it would interfere with Daddy hearing the radio. He did have some hearing deficit from being around noisy machinery, I suppose. The bedroom wall was directly behind where he sat next to his radio and our bunk beds were on the side of the room directly behind him. It was often that one by one, oldest first, we were called out of the bedroom for a spanking. We finally learned to cry soon so he would stop sooner. I think the first ones got the hardest spankings.

As we all lay in our beds sniffling I, being more of a rascal, would say," I'll bet Daddy's hand stings."

That would make someone beside me chuckle. Oleta would whisper for us to be quiet or we would get it again. After a moment of soft sobs I would say something about Daddy's hand being as big as that of Paul Bunyan and muffled chuckles were heard again. Being sad was no fun. On

144

occasion I might query something like if the others knew why Paul's ox, Babe, was blue. Someone would always ask why, usually Charlene.

I said, "It was because it was blue from getting smacked just like our biscuits."

Oleta would put her hand over my mouth as I chuckled under my blanket. I just had a hard time unwinding after a full day of activity. Sometimes I would make up a story and tell it to the others. In a loud whisper Oleta would tell me to whisper lower and the rest to listen louder. We had fun sometimes when we were supposed to be sleeping. It just seemed like more fun than it did in the daytime. I am speaking for myself here lest I incriminate an innocent one among us. We finally went to sleep with tears on our pillows and smiles on our faces. I saw it as making the best out of not even reasonably good circumstances.

I remember one thing that Charlene and I did that was fun in the daytime. We found a board about eight feet long and took it up to the hay mow. We lifted it high enough Charlene's feet would still be in the hay when she sat on the board. It was the same ladder I used to crawl on the two by six board twenty feet off the ground to get to the bird's nest. Mama told us to never crawl on that board and we never did. She didn't say to never make a teeter totter on the rungs. We ran the board through the rung so it was extending on each side of the ladder about equal distance, with my end a little shorter. I went on the outside where there was a lot of air between me and the ground. I wanted to let go of the rung above the one the board was on, but I wasn't sure Charlene could keep the board from slipping as I was heavier than she so I held on the rung. Charlene would push hard with her legs and we teetered on the board quite a while. We never told Mama. I believed like she did that some things were better left unsaid.

I remember when Wesley was little that he liked to go to the woods with us and pick flowers. It was a long walk for him and his little legs got tired so I often carried him piggy back. When we came back his little chubby legs were more tired than ever so he would sit in the lane and cry when I put him down. His cute face was mud-smeared all around his big brown eyes. He wanted me to carry him so I would rest a little, then pick him up and carry him some more. It was about a half mile from the woods to the house. One day, I found my old worn out doll buggy an old pig house we had made into a playhouse. I took the wheels off and put them on the bottom of a crate and tied a rope to it and pulled little Wes in it until it fell apart. Our Radio Flyer red wagon was long worn out, but we could always find something to do.

I liked having a pole in my hand and walking on the wooden pig fence. It wobbled as I walked and was a challenge but I never fell in with the pigs. They dug up the yard in the barnyard and after it rained, they loved to wallow and lie in the mud. It must have kept them cool. They liked their backs scratched so sometimes I would scratch them with my pole. They grunted happily as if in hog Heaven. The smaller ones would try to root under the fence and get out of their pen. Daddy put rings in their noses to keep them from doing it as it must have hurt to dig. They reacted like a cat with its tail caught in a door when Daddy put the sharp rings in their noses. I felt sorry for the young animals that didn't know better.

As we grew older there was plenty of work for us to do helping Daddy with farm chores. Sometimes we would milk cows. My cow was Daisy, a gentle smallish Jersey. Charlene's was a big Holstein that kicked sometimes. She had to put chains around its back legs so it couldn't kick and hit her and knock her off the three legged stool and spill the milk. Charlene was a brave girl. The other cows were pretty docile. When Charlene and I helped each other we were strong enough to handle a gunny sack full of heavy wheat. Our job was to keep a bag on both feeders so one could fill and the empty one was kept ready. We had to change the flow of the grain as a bag was full, quickly tie it off with cut pieces of binder twine like Daddy taught us and kick it out on a slide and off the combine where the bags were collected later. We had to tie them correctly so they wouldn't open when they fell. Daddy ran the combine with his tractor. It was hard work for us girls and we never worked this task together as there wasn't room. I was usually the one Daddy called on first; as Charlene grew bigger she took over. We built up pretty good muscles for girls. We drove tractor at plowing time when Daddy was doing others things and that was fun. Oleta preferred being indoors more so she stayed inside and helped Mama; although I believe she did drive tractor a bit.

One year Daddy planted an acre of canning pickles to sell. Picking them was a big job and they had to be picked at least every third day as they needed to be picked when they were small and worth more money. I think all of us kids worked on that project, even Mama at times. We kids hoped to earn enough money for a bicycle. By then Oleta, Charlene and I were in high school. Patricia and Wesley shared a used bike for school. We never got to use the bike we earned very much. Our parents just couldn't afford one for each of us, in fact, not even one to share when we were younger.

We walked when the weather allowed. I remember there were a few times Daddy had to come get us from school with the tractor as the roads were too deep with snow for a car to get through. All the kids who lived in houses we passed or lived near the corner where kids lived on the other road came with us and Daddy dropped them off along the way. It was a fun experience for the kids. Our tractor barely got through the deep snow. One time our teacher couldn't get home and stayed overnight with the older couple next door. Mama stayed over with her parents as she taught near them. Schools almost never closed after a blizzard started once school was open for the day. It seems there is always a way to deal with whatever circumstances present.

I was probably eleven years old when freezer lockers became available for rent at the grocery store in Ithaca. One could bring in their fresh-butchered meat and have the store butchers cut it up, wrap, and label it. Our parents brought in beef as it was an economical way to preserve it and it didn't need to be canned. It was great for fresh frozen strawberries and other foods like corn, green beans, and other good foods. Mama brought in cases of foods in quart freezer containers made from waxed cardboard. No more awful canned almost albino looking strawberries which is how all canned ones looked. I remember that the big cold room smelled with a pleasant and sort of sweet aroma. Our nostrils stuck closed after we were in the room for awhile. I was glad to know there was a bell a person could ring if they couldn't open the nearly foot-thick door. We were thrilled by the use of a freezer. Sometimes we each could buy a nickel's worth of treats while Mama picked up a few groceries and other things. It was fun to go to the dime store. Finances were slowly getting a little better for us and we were so grateful.

Chapter 24

1946

Though winter was coming to a close it gave one last and furious blast of the season this year. It began with a blizzard during the night that continued this morning and it was a school day for Mama and all of her children. Daddy drove to check the roads after milking the cows and felt if Mama took the route he selected she could make it to school. It was not usual for schools to close in bad weather. We three girls who were now in high school were waiting for our school bus. Normally we walked a third mile to the corner. With the cold wind blowing so badly our bus driver attempted to pick us up at our house. We were always well behaved on the bus so he liked us and we liked him as well.

A low area in the road beyond our property line near where the ice pond was had become deep in water following the start of a spring thaw only days ago. Unfortunately, during the night and into the morning the water froze. The school bus became stuck in broken ice and frigid water so Daddy went down the road with the tractor to pull it out. I went out and stood against our new house seeking shelter as I watched Daddy try to pull the bus out of the mess. After a few minutes it appeared he was making little progress so I started toward the little house to report the problem.

As I was on my way, I noticed smoke billowing out under the eaves of our new house. I was stunned. I jerked open the door of the little house. Mama was just putting on her coat to go to the car and start for school. I yelled that the new house was on fire. Mama took a quick look and called for Oleta to run across the road and have the neighbors call the fire department. I said I would run to get Daddy. I ran down the road yelling and waving my arms but Daddy couldn't hear or see me. As I got closer, he saw me and saw the smoke that was not visible earlier because of the blowing snow. In seconds he jumped in the icy water and unhooked the tractor. I started running home. The bus was left sitting in the middle of the road and other neighbors finally came with their tractors to pull it out of the mess.

In the excitement, while on the phone, the neighbor lady did not instruct the firemen to bring the truck the back way to our house and avoid the deep hole in the road. Oleta hadn't thought of it either. As soon as the neighbor lady was off the phone she noticed a pool of blood at my sister's feet and on her kitchen floor. She asked Oleta what happened and she said she fell on jagged ice and must have cut her knee on the way to their house. She said it was hurting some. The neighbor lady examined it and said it was a bad jagged deep cut and probably needed to be sutured. She told Oleta to stay where she was and she would send one of the girls over to tell Mama and see if she wanted a doctor called. She kindly offered Oleta a chair and cleaned up her leg around the wound and the floor. Mama told the older neighbor girl who came to see what Mama wanted done to have her mother call our doctor and see if he could come out to tend to Oleta. She ran back to tell her mother which doctor Mama wanted. It was the same one who had removed the bullet from my arm. He knew where we lived. He had delivered some of Mama's babies in the little house. She told the doctor our new house was on fire. He expressed great sorrow and said he would come right out. It was over six miles as our neighbor lady remembered to tell him to come the back way as the bus was stuck in the broken ice and water and to pick her up at the house across the road. When he arrived he saw the bus gone, but the fire truck stuck in the icy mess while smoked billowed from our new house. The doctor was horrified. The neighbor's who had gotten the bus out had come on the run to help fight the fire. Nobody was there at the corner to tell the fire truck driver to take the other route. The firemen could see the fire and came racing around the corner onto our road towards our house. They had no idea how deep the hole in the road was. The firemen found when they finally were helped out from being stuck that the fire hose had broken off and they needed to return to town to get it fixed. They called the Middleton fire department which was further away than Ithaca. Our doctor took Oleta back to his office and said he would bring her back.

News about our new house burning spread fast. Men came from both directions in vehicles and then on the run by foot to help do whatever they could. One man walked from across the section through snow over his knees as he couldn't get his car out of his driveway. People all around the area had watched the house building progress as Daddy built it alone and were stunned to learn it was burning.

The first thing Daddy did, after leaving the bus and speeding to our house, was grab the slop bucket from the little house that contained water, potato, apple peels, and whey for feeding the pigs. He ran to the back door of the new house as I opened the door for him. Daddy ran inside taking the four steps up to the main floor in two steps. He stepped a few feet closer and forcefully flung the contents at the top of the large floor register just above the furnace. He had the flooring drying above the register and stacked on two saw horses. For some reason the blower did not come on and the flooring became too hot and started to burn. With one swift kick Daddy knocked the sawhorses out from under the stacked wood in hopes of delaying the spread of the fire as the flooring would land together in a pile on top of the register. I had followed him inside and stood back from the flames and rushed out ahead of him to open the door.

When Daddy raced out of the house with singed eyebrows and his hat and mackinaw singed he slammed the windowed back door too hard and the glass shattered. He reached in the snow and cooled his gloves and the cap he was wearing with the ear flaps down. He went on the run for a piece of metal to cover the door where the pane was missing as the draft from the broken window was fanning the fire. Daddy quickly found a piece of metal and nailed it over the window while, I helped him hold it.

The neighbor lady considerately took it upon herself to put out word to the right people, that the school where Mama taught would be closed for the day. She asked that word be passed on to as many families as possible to prevent people from struggling to get there only to find it closed.

We four girls had our new furniture already in our bedrooms. With two sharing the room there was a double bed, mattress and springs, a chest of drawers and a vanity with a stool in each of the two bedrooms. Two neighbors had climbed a ladder and gone into the upstairs through a window kids had broken out with snowballs, but needed to do more destruction to get furniture out. They got every piece of furniture out through the window and other men caught each piece before they hit the ground; not even the mirrors were broken. They were wonderful help. One of the men fell through the floor, was injured and needed to be seen by a doctor. Just as the doctor returned with Oleta, Daddy alerted him that a neighbor man was injured and needed a doctor. He looked him over, took him into town, treated him, and brought him back. Daddy told him to bill us and thanked the doctor for all he had done and was doing to help. Oleta had several stitches in her knee and a thick bandage covered the area. She walked stiff legged for several days and was left with a jagged scar just under the knee cap.

Men galore were standing by in case our little house would need to be emptied, and maybe the animals in the barn and pig house as well. The fire got closer as the wind carried it. Our school bus driver was among them as he never completed his route. He had watched the house go up as Daddy built it and was sick about the fire. By the time the Middleton fire department arrived they determined they needed more help and called the Alma fire department, which had to come from about twice the distance they had come. Not long afterwards, the Ithaca fire truck was back to help. It looked like the little house, barn and all the farm buildings were vulnerable to catching fire so there was plenty to do for the firemen from three trucks. The fire burned for four hours. Daddy had put fire stops in the walls and that was why much of the house still stood after the fire was out. The firemen were amazed.

We had been using the laundry facilities in the basement of the new house as they were modern and much more convenient than what we tolerated for so many years in the little house. The laundry equipment in the basement corner was amazingly still functional but black with smoke.

After the fire was out the damage could be assessed. Until we actually lived in the house, insurance would not cover the damages. The once beautiful plaster was black and in a heap on the furnace and on the floors and in the basement where the fire had burned through the dining room floors. The large dining room window on the end was burned away and the glass destroyed. The front windows needed replacing. Some of the bedroom Oleta and I were to share was missing part of the floor as it was above the dining room. There was a lot of repair work to be done.

I can still envision Daddy sitting on the open stairway and staring as though he was figuring just how he would repair everything and figuring where to start first with all that needed doing. I felt so sorry for him after all his labor in building us all a nice house. He had planted Chinese elm trees in the front lawn as they were beautiful and very fast growing. We were all grateful that the ornamental and shade trees survived the fire.

Daddy replaced the windows first. The end ones in the dining room had to be larger than before as the wood around them had burned through the outer wall. He put in many small paned windows that covered much of the end of the dining room except a window seat he added. He also added a built-in china cupboard on one end of the window with a bookcase and desk combination at the other. Daddy repaired the floor joists and ceilings next as needed. It took him a few days to shovel out the plaster and other debris. The walls and ceilings all had to be refinished or replaced. There were places where woodwork had to be replaced. All the rest had to be cleaned or sanded and refinished. It took us children weeks to help get the sanding done.

By November of the same year we moved in just before Thanksgiving Day. We had much to be thankful for on Thanksgiving. The smell of smoke always remained in the attic and it was black from smoke but we didn't notice unless the attic was open. We were just so excited about living in a house with plenty of room that it seemed a minor detail after all we had been through. Shortly after Thanksgiving we had our first Christmas tree in our house. Decorating was so much fun. What a grand thrill it was for us all. I had spent fourteen years and four months in the little and Oleta had spent another year and two months. Our parents lived there a year longer or just over sixteen incredible years.

It was our parent's intention and determination to do all that was necessary so we could live in that house. They had overcome years of obstacles by their willingness to work hard and make many sacrifices. I believe we probably were right where God wanted us and if that is the case I have no regrets. In fact, all we experienced may have saved us from being less compassionate people than we are today. I think it is possible that many people don't realize their blessings until years later. They don't always immediately see a blessing totally for what it really is. Perhaps, since we don't see the whole picture, we need to be more accepting of situations in our lives that seem like negatives. They may have purpose in our lives. It may be to deal with and overcome them with good reason. Since we have finite minds it means we are not always going to understand what God has done. Giving Him the benefit of the doubt seems a practical approach. What do we have to lose by trusting Him? I don't like hearing people say "It is God's will" when bad things happen. I in no way blame God for bad things that happen in our lives. They are usually caused by human error be it accidental or of carelessness, bad choices, or even curses.

Sometimes it seems that the wrong person is punished like in the case of an accident the other created. God allows his natural laws to prevail. I am not saying that He never intervenes as in the case of faith with prayer. It has been proven many times that He does. He gives us free will so we are not like puppets or robots. He leaves the choice up to us about how we live our lives, but sees to it we are offered instruction for our own sake. He wants us to have abundant lives when in our physical bodies and blissful ones in the hereafter. We can either accept His instruction and promises or reject them.

We, who believe His Word and accept it, need to help others to do the same. It can sometimes be by example. There is no doubt we all have purpose in our God given lives. It behooves us to recognize that.

I desire to let it be known in this book that we have never forgotten the money that was collected by the Mennonite people and others to help us with our loss. May God richly bless all. Our doctor is no longer alive, but he was a wonderful man who never sent us a bill for his services that day. People like this make the world a better place to live. Sometimes it is a small thing that makes a big difference in others lives. Every cent in a dollar is what helps creates it. Who knows what even a smile might do for someone. The beauty of it is that it takes less energy than a frown.

Chapter 25

Tragedy Strikes

One of my Daddy's best friends taught shop class where my brother attended Fulton high school. Wesley was particularly good friends with one of the teacher's sons. They both enjoyed fishing and hunting together. Wesley was fifteen years old when he was burnishing a broken fishing spear in preparation for the brazing process. His teacher stepped out of the room for a moment. The spinning wire brush grabbed the spear and rammed one tine in Wesley's eye knocking him over backward and part way across the room. It pulled his eye out from its socket and it lay attached to the spear. The aqueous and vitreous humor inside the eyeball was running out and the eyeball was collapsing. The other students were shocked at what they saw. Some stayed near him and others ran from the room frantically yelling for their teacher. He came running in to a terrible scene. The teacher hastily sent a couple of students to run quickly and tell the superintendent and principal to rush to the classroom. He dismissed the others to study hall. In minutes the local doctor was administering an injection of morphine to Wesley. He said Wesley needed to be taken by ambulance to Sparrow Hospital in Lansing immediately where he knew of a good eye surgeon who was affiliated with the hospital. The teacher told the principal he would go to the school where Wesley's mother was teaching and drive her to Lansing to be with her son. As soon as he arrived and surprised my mother, he told her to dismiss school as he needed to take her to Lansing where Wes was being taken to the hospital.

He drove my mother the fifty miles from her school to the hospital. My father received a phone call regarding the situation. I had trained in Sparrow Hospital then affiliated with Michigan State University so I knew several of the doctors and my way around the hospital. My husband and I quickly rushed to pick up my father. He was so upset that he was unable to find one dress shoe. He didn't realize he had knocked something down in the closet that covered his shoe. We were off in a moment heading for Lansing which was about fifty miles from my parent's home and about seventy from ours.

Wesley was sleeping when we arrived. The doctor had seen him and said he would do surgery within the hour. He gave no guarantees that he could save Wesley's eye. After surgery he told us he found it necessary to put in an artificial eye. He said Wesley would be able to turn it as he had attached it to his eye muscles. Then he explained that Wesley was very fortunate because a second tine had hit just above his other eye on the frontal bone and missed piercing it by about a quarter of an inch but had penetrated an inch and close to the brain. It was very nearly an even greater disaster. Wesley developed infection in his eye and the muscles deteriorated. The artificial eye had to be removed and a different one put in using another method of attachment that allowed no movement. The area had to heal before the glass piece that fit on the front of the prosthesis could be inserted. He was hospitalized for sixteen days.

When Wesley returned to school everyone felt badly for him as he wore a black patch over his eye socket while the area healed and shrunk back enough for a proper fit. Not only were my parents and the rest of the family sick about his terrible tragedy, but so was his teacher. The two families remained friends. Wesley had problems with a mucous discharge that needed clearing away on occasion and the glass eye felt uncomfortably cold in cold weather. He didn't complain about his glass eye feeling cold; it was just his response when asked. He often needed to wipe his eye and the mucus problem was evident without him mentioning it. The match with his good eye was excellent. However, with only one eye it was not safe for him to be farming. He needed a less hazardous job and after years of college became an aquatic biologist.

He was very successful in the field and was asked to go to Poland and help with water problems. He was also asked to go to Valdez, Alaska and help solve the problem the oil spill had created. He needed to come up with a bacterium that would eat the stuff from the water. Various articles he wrote were published regarding his field of work. With persuasion he eventually taught at a university that needed his knowledge and expertise in his field. He worked in almost every state in the United States. Being a fun person, he sometimes would pull the front piece of his artificial eye out and allow it to look at an opponent's hand when in a family card game. He almost never mentioned his compromised visibility. With diligence Wesley learned to compensate for his changed depth perception when he was hunting as well as adjust to a reduced peripheral vision. I never heard him complain. He was determined to make the best of a less than desirable situation and bravely accomplished it.

Chapter 26

A Diversion

Lifestyles of generations in America are always different from the preceding one. Some changes result from new scientific discoveries, war, the economy, new inventions, lack of religion and changes of mores and new laws. Like human relationships they never remain static but change in varied degrees. Some people very much resist change. With others, change is so insidious they are almost unaware it is happening. In the story that follows it is my intention to show the difficulty of some people to make change; but that change can bring positive results. This story is of my own imagination, but based somewhat on the life of a family I became acquainted with in the late seventies. It offers an interesting and inspirational outcome.

Dominick's type-A personality is far from covert. He is always impeccably dressed right down to his spotless and well shined shoes. Keeping up with the latest men's fashions for business men and his well styled and cut hair seem the only change he tolerates. He is a tall, handsome specimen of a man. Dark suits and snow-white shirts very well ironed enhanced his black wavy hair and beautiful white teeth and olive complexion. He is fully aware his ties that contain blue that match his stunning eyes produce just the right results. As CEO of a fairly young, rapidly growing company, he deems it critical that his appearance befit his work position. People who know him well realize there are other reasons. He is always at his office by exactly 9:00 a.m. in the morning and out at 5:00 p.m. in the afternoon. His desk is always neat and in perfect order when he arrives and leaves. When possible, and he can usually arrange that, he begins his exercise routine exactly at noon. It takes place in his private suite next to his office. Between 12:25 p.m. and 12:40 p.m. he showers, combs his hair, and gets back into his office attire. At exactly 12:45 p.m. he eats his catered in lunch and brushes his teeth immediately afterward. By 1:10 p.m. he is always back in his office looking and smelling fresh.

His wife, Meeky, realizes with all the demands he puts on her that she has developed what she calls a Cinderella Complex. She never wears slippers nor has ever even seen a glass one, or a prince. All she has come to know are hours of drudgery. She was an executive secretary until shortly after their marriage. She wore befitting business suits and kept herself neat and looking professional. She was single, naturally beautiful with light blond well kept hair, creamy complexion and with very green eyes enhanced by mascara on her long lashes. When Dominick began his pursuit of her he was often in the office where she worked for another CEO. He knew how to pour on the charm.

Within a year they married. It wasn't long after their marriage before Dominick asked her to quit her work outside the home. She liked her job and made good money so she explained that if they had children she would stay at home. It wasn't long after that statement Meeky learned they were going to have twins. They were born a year and two months after their marriage. Sixteen months later a third child was added to the family. It seemed apparent that her husband was going to see to it that Meeky did not work outside the home. The family lived in a large and lovely home in an upper class neighborhood. Dominick made it clear to his wife that he expected it to be kept spotless as he wanted it to be his haven of rest. He told her that because he earned a good income that he felt worthy. In his usual expostulate manner he said he expected good homemade meals. He expected her to keep the kitchen spotless and well supplied with food and his favorite drinks. He told her he expected his children to always be clean and neatly attired.

He made it clear that when he was in his den he expected the children not to interrupt him while he had his beer, read the mail and newspaper and watched his favorite television programs. His den was his pleasant re-treat and Meeky dusted it every day as she was told to do. The big leather recliner chair has a table lamp with a matching leather base. It sits upon a lovely cherry wood table with a leather insert on top that matches the lamp. A set of coasters is always in exactly the same place on the table top. Dominick has a cherry wood magazine rack where Meeky is to leave his daily mail and newspaper. A large television is located directly across the room from his chair. Dominick's long leather sofa matches his brownish-red leather chair and sits out away from a large bookcase. Each end holds lovely contrasting throw pillows; one with a lion's head and the other a leopard's head. Lovely tables of matching cherry wood and leather inserts are of a different size and shape from the table next to his chair and are at each end of the sofa. A pair of brass lamps rest on the two tables. The room has a very elegant masculine motif. It is not uncommon for Dominick to run his finger over door tops when he is near one anywhere in the house. He always inspects for dust and if he finds any, Meeky hears about it. He is not going to be the one to clean off the dust. Meeky is petite and it is all she can do to reach the door tops with a feather duster. Her husband is not allergic to dust; he simply refuses to dust yet is insistent on no dust in the house. Dominick seems to be a narcissistic, neurotic, obsessive-compulsive, inflexible, domineering and demanding self centered man. His wife tolerates him, but not without it affecting her attitude about how she sees herself.

One cannot escape the thought that being meek and domineering befit their names well. She would be better off with being less meek and he with being less domineering. Dominick expects his dinner served at 5:45 p.m. every evening right after he finishes his cold beer. Meeky always has her work cut out. After dinner is over she often is swamped with all that needs doing. Dominick does not ever want his children in the den. The children soon understand it is simply out of bounds.

He expects Meeky to rear the children and care for them by herself. In the evening she bathes them, helps them brush their teeth, gets them ready for bed and reads them a story. When a child has a new toy and wants to show it to Daddy, he takes a quick look and with little to no response pleasing to the child, he tells the child to put it away neatly when done using it and walks away. Meeky has taught the children to pick up their toys and put them away when they are done playing with them, so that is done before they get ready for bed. It seems the children have no chance other than becoming duplicate personalities of their father. Meeky is well aware of it and tries to find ways to prevent that from happening; no easy task.

After letting the children play a while in the tub, Meeky has a bathroom to clean up and towels and washcloths to hang neatly. She tries to iron while the children are in bed so she won't have to be concerned they might bump the ironing board and knock the iron off it. Dominick demands clean well-ironed shirts daily so he can select the white shirt of his choice. There is never much time for conversation between the couple. Dominick had conversations with adults most of his working day and he doesn't want much of it after getting home from work. He gives no consideration that his wife has mainly spoken with the children or to a dog all day.

Meeky is glad their youngest child is sleeping all night. Before that, going to bed seemed more like time-out. Her days begin at 5:30 a.m. six days a week. She puts on her jogging clothes when first arising. Next she makes coffee, puts fresh water in the dog's bowl, and takes Pamper out for his morning run. Except for winter months, she enjoys the fresh air and change of exercise from her household duties. When she returns from their run she feeds Pamper his allotted amount of dog food and refills the dog's water bowl. Dominick doesn't get up until 8:00 a.m. Meeky cherishes her few quiet minutes to enjoy her coffee as she makes up her list of duties for the day. Sometimes she prepares homemade muffins to serve her husband for breakfast. Each day of the week she prepares something homemade that is different, nourishing and tasty for him. The children are always up and eating breakfast before Dominick leaves for work at exactly 8:50 a.m. There is no time for morning conversation between the couple. Meeky has shrunk from a size eight to a four since she married Dominick. Soon after she quit working outside the home he had her gather up her nice suits and other things that no longer fit her and he took them to Goodwill. She now wears a muumuu everyday while working around the house. It is in the small category, but styled close to a one-size-fits-all garment. She has few other clothes that fit. Easy on and off items accommodate her lifestyle. Daily she wears her plastic apron over her muumuus.

By the time she can go to bed, Meeky can barely wait to get in the shower and wash her hair and feel the warm water running down her achy back. The plastic apron she wears often causes her to perspire heavily. She has not enjoyed a relaxing soaking bath in years. There never is any adult aromatherapy bubble bath on her grocery list. The last time she had a bubble bath was when she discovered their youngest child in the children's pool lying face down. It was not easy to spot the baby as one of the twins had dumped the rest of the bubble bath in the bottle into the pool. Meeky jumped in, grabbed the little one and sat her up, leaned her forward and compressed her lung area and out came the water. She had heard it was a good way to handle such a situation and it worked for her. The baby seemed to be okay, but needed to be quickly checked over and the fastest way was to call an ambulance. Meeky's only bubble bath since marriage was as over as soon as it started and wasn't any fun. The baby survived with no ill effects for which Meeky was so grateful. Neither she nor her husband would ever have forgiven her had the tragedy cost the child her life or was her brain damaged.

One night as Meeky was ready to take her bedtime shower, she noticed an image in the full length mirror. It was appalling to her. She realized she even looked like Cinderella did in her daily clothes. Her plastic apron, muumuu, plastic shoes, and scarf on her head tied behind her ears and under the scarf's corner were a frightful scene. She noticed how red and ugly her hands looked. Her nails were very short unlike when she worked in the office. She saw herself as a disgusting mess. She had resorted to the plastic apron and shoes because she mopped the kitchen, baths and laundry room floors every day. She often watered the garden and shampooed and dried the dog and she always got wet when she gave the children their baths.

Going to bed beat and feeling down, she hoped only for a good night's sleep. Getting off her tired legs would feel so good. She was in no mood for anything but sleep. Complaining of a headache, which she had, would do no good as her husband would simply ignore it. Dominick enjoyed going to the office and looked forward to coming home to his haven of rest while

Meeky's work was never done. She lived where she worked and could never escape seeing something that needed doing.

One day her husband called her from work asking that she bring him the camera. He said he needed it in fifteen minutes. It was an easy eight minutes from his office to the house but Meeky was in the middle of mopping floors. She needed to stop and change clothes and clean up a bit before she drove to the office after gathering up her three children. His asking her to bring the camera disgusted her. Nevertheless, she placed all the children in their car seats and made certain they were secure before she drove off to the office. She told the children she just needed to run in and hand their daddy the camera and she would come right out. On arriving at the office parking lot she told them if they were well behaved and left the car doors locked she would buy them an ice cream cone. She was not concerned as they had learned well to follow directions.

Little did she or her husband know what the results of her trip to the office would bring. He had timed her expected visit so the secretary would be on her break when she arrived. When Meeky arrived at her husband's office the door was barely ajar and Meeky could see he was talking with a man from across his desk. She turned to see if she could leave the camera with his secretary just as she walked back into her office. She had forgotten her makeup kit and that was why she was back at the time. Meeky got the shock of her life. Her husband's secretary looked like a Manhattan streetwalker. Her skirt was short; her boots long, and heels high. Now Meeky understood why he almost never mentioned her. She looked like Dolly Parton's twin from her bleached blond hair to the bottom of her boots. Above her high cut skirt was low cut spaghetti-strap top. It didn't come close to qualifying as a blouse. Her glitzy bright red jacket matched her mini skirt, but was hanging on a wall peg near her desk. It wasn't even very warm in the office or outside. Had Miss Floozy Secretary leaned forward, two masses of adipose tissue would have oozed out like toothpaste from its tube. Meeky found it tempting to drop the car keys to see if she would bend down to pick them up, but couldn't decide if she wanted to check

Miss Floozy Secretary's partially exposed cheeks for color or the fat balls for color so didn't try the experiment.

Since it was early spring in Michigan the tanning weather hadn't begun. It was certain that her husband's secretary spent a lot of time at the tanning salon. She had a gorgeous tan everywhere visible, that being almost all over. Her long legs above her boots looked almost roasted and smooth as her satin top. It seemed natural to wonder where her tan ended. Meeky was sure her husband wondered every day—unless he already knew. Meeky was sure the floozy's legs were bare. Meeky also deduced that Miss Floozy Secretary was tanned all over. Bending over and exposing white cheeks would just be too tacky for a gal with perfect nails, long black artificial eyelashes, a Dolly Parton hairdo, and makeup that must be touched up at least three times a day at her breaks.

Her desk was placed straight across the hall from the desk of Meeky's husband where they faced each other, but her desk had no backing at the knee hole. That is what her husband viewed every day. Meeky was livid when she left the office. She couldn't even remember if she handed the camera to Miss Floozy Secretary. It was no longer in her hand so she decided she must have. At the moment it was not a prime concern. The children were fine and she drove directly to get them an ice cream cone. She decided to have one, too. Since she couldn't lick her wounds, she could get some comfort from licking a cone. She was glad each of the children was licking one as she was not in the mood to talk. She needed to think. She was sure that with her husband knowing his wife had finally met his secretary he would be anxious *about* coming home rather than anxious *to* come home. She was sure her scheme would totally confound her husband. It would take place in the immediate early evening. Meeky decided it would be perfect timing as the children were to be picked up in a half hour to stay overnight with her parents. She was anxious to make preparations for putting it into action. Suddenly, another thought flashed across her mind. This one would happen tomorrow night and be the big shocker for her husband. Her emotions of anger were quickly being replaced with excitement.

The children had their three pieces of luggage waiting in the front entry area for their grandparents. Meeky's parents didn't stay long as the children were anxious to spend time at their house and see what new toys awaited their visit. There was always something new every time they went. They loved all the attention their grandpa and grandma gave them. They barely even talked to their daddy and rarely even saw much of him. Meeky thought the timing in meeting Miss Floozy Secretary could not have been better. She thought it very interesting that his secretary forgot to take her makeup kit with her. She saw it as an omen that it was meant to be just as it turned out.

As soon as Meeky was alone she cried. In a moment she was feeling a bit giddy and found herself laughing. She decided something had to be done to bring about a change. She felt her scheme was a good start. The more she thought about her scheme the better she felt. She finally sat down and laughed until tears ran down her legs. She didn't care as she decided not to mention Miss Floozy Secretary this evening. She knows he will be wondering when she is going to mention her. It will be fun to watch her husband squirm and try to avoid her all evening even with the children gone. She was not going to make it easy for him. That was part of her first scheme.

She planned to fix an elaborate meal this evening to eat in the candle-lit dining room. She deems she needs to bake a pie and get things ready for a nice meal. Meeky set the table with their best china, sterling silverware, and two crystal wine pieces of stemware set on a linen tablecloth. Just before her husband arrives home she plans to pick lilacs and ferns for a centerpiece that will encircle a large white candle that she will later light. She is going to knock his socks right down to his slippers. He won't know what to think. A sardonic grin suddenly appears on her face. While making the pie she begins to think about what will be involved in pulling off her second scheme. She knows what she will fix for dinner and what she will have to do when. As soon as she is done with the pie she will make a list of everything she will need for tomorrow.

Her plan is to be dressed exactly like Miss Floozy Secretary when her husband arrives home after work. She has a story to tell him that will be as shocking as her appearance. She will tell her husband that she got a call from Mr. Hunk, the fellow she worked for until her husband insisted she quit. She will tell Dominick he said he had an offer for her that would be very difficult to turn down. She will also tell him she is to meet Mr. Hunk at 6:00 p.m. at the Heavenly Supper Club at the corner of Paradise and Passion. Then she will say she needs to leave immediately. At that moment she will hand her husband a list of things to accomplish while she is gone that she will refer to it as a note. It will be folded in fourths so it can't be opened quickly.

Before her husband has time to collect his wits, she will be out the door and into her car. She will make a list of all the duties she will *tell*, not *ask* him to do. At the bottom she will tell him she just did not have time to get everything done as she had a very busy day. It will be a very long list. She will actually go to a movie that she heard was hilarious. An almost wicked laugh arose at the thought of her plans. She needed to make a list of items she hoped to pick up at Goodwill or The Salvation Army thrift stores. She would need one quick stop at the grocery store.

Her list read:
- FLOOZIE FROCKS
- White satin spaghetti strap top
- Bright red mini skirt (no jacket)
- Black tall shiny boots
- Lacy thirty-two DD bra
- Blond full wig
- Bronze body, face makeup
- Long black artificial eyelashes, glue
- Long bright red artificial nails, glue
- Two large oranges or small grapefruit, equal sizes

Laughing all the way to her closet, Meeky placed the list in the pocket of her black spring coat. As she put some tissues in the other pocket, she found a ten dollar bill. It would buy her movie ticket and dinner which would be all the hot buttered popcorn she could eat chased by colas. She saw the money as a second sign that all was going to go well in pulling off her schemes. It encouraged her in thinking that there would surely be favorable results after all was said and done. She grabbed her coat and loafers and put them in her car. They would be there tomorrow with the ten dollars in her coat pocket. She would cover her Floozy frocks with her coat and replace her boots with her loafers, then pull off her wig and brush her simple Dorothy Hamill hairdo with the brush she always carried in her purse for the children's hair. It would be done before arriving at the theater. Sunglasses would hide her long lashes as she bought her ticket and popcorn and first cola. She didn't want to spend a lot of money on Floozy frocks, but she would do what was necessary. It occurred to her that she could wear the foolish costume to the annual neighborhood New Year's Eve party. Maybe she could even win the prize like last year when she wore her Freudian slip as a dress. A tag dangled from its upper back with it reading: Freudian Slips make no mistakes. She smiled as she well remembered it was a big hit at the party. Her brain synapses were almost on overload. An adrenaline rush made her feel she could nearly fly. She told herself she needed to calm down and get dinner finished. It wasn't easy to prepare a lavish meal while her thoughts were elsewhere, but she did it exactly as planned.

Dominick arrived home at his usual time and was ready to eat at 5:45 p.m. as usual. He was surprised when Meeky told him the two of them would have dinner in the dining room since the children weren't home. Her husband stood in astonishment as he viewed the table and heard the soft dinner music.

With a big smile he said, "Now this is more like it. A meal with atmosphere with no children to spoil it."

A feeling of hostility suddenly rushed through Meeky, but she enjoyed the appreciation of her efforts; it was so rare she could barely believe he said it. The thought flashed across her mind that maybe Dominick should have never had children. It disgusted her that he was so self absorbed. After a few sips of wine with no conversation, Meeky got up from the table, excused herself saying she would be right back and returned with a sterling tray holding two colorful leafy salads and a basket of hot buttered garlic bread. She removed the food from the tray and placed them in the appropriate places and sat the tray on the buffet and herself at the table. Her husband commented on how great the bread smelled and suggested eating it while it was hot. They each indulged along with their salad. Only a little bread was left. Meeky again got up and cleared the salad bowls and forks away and with the tray went back to the kitchen. This time she returned with two plates that held a filet mignon, a baked half-sweet potato that was fluffed in its shell and dripping with honey butter with a hint of ginger. Asparagus spears lay on one side of the plate and were streaked with hollandaise sauce. After he had taken a few bites, her husband said it was almost too attractive to eat, but he said he found the taste surpassed the beauty. He offered a smile and she smiled and thanked him. Soon she was returning with the tray carrying one large and one small piece of thick chocolate pie with whipped cream swirled high on the top. Two mint leaves lay together on one side of each pie plate. A hot cup of coffee was placed near each plate. Everything she fixed was eaten.

Meeky was observing her husband in quick glances throughout the meal. She knew he was wondering what was to happen next. Dominick offered little eye contact. He stood up as soon as he was done eating and collected everything from the table except the centerpiece, and put it all on the tray and carried it into the kitchen. Meeky was aghast, but kept herself under control. She sensed he was anxious to be by himself in the den. She carefully cleared off the table cloth and napkins after blowing out the candle and turning off the music. On her way to the laundry room her husband stopped her, gave her a kiss on the lips and thanked her for a delicious meal in such a serene setting with no noisy children. What he said was bittersweet to her ears. She appreciated his thanking her and reference of a delicious meal, but was beginning to think that she was right, Dominick should never have had children. The thought had occurred to her a few times in the past, but he made direct reference to the children interfering with life two times just in the evening. It really reaffirmed her suspicion and she felt sad about it.

Meeky loved her precious children and suspected that her parents occasionally picked them up knowing her husband spent almost no time with them. She knew they were aware she worked very hard and needed a break. Dominick had retreated to his den as she cleaned up the dishes and kitchen. Meeky thought he didn't even take the time for one slow dance.

As soon as she was done with kitchen work she sat in her seldom used easy chair in the living room and compiled her list of chores for Dominick tomorrow night. Little did he know she wouldn't be fixing him dinner tomorrow night. She muffled a chuckle as the thought crossed her mind. She had nearly completed the list in about a half hour. She thought of a few more things she could add as she wrote. It was a very long list just as she had planned. She put it in her muumuu pocket and thought the list was serving her well as she was venting her hostilities without saying a word. She thought actions spoke louder than words and he was going to see that tomorrow evening. Her muffled laugh was one she seldom heard. Leisurely, she thumbed through some outdated unopened catalogs for a while. She was not accustomed to being able to sit in a lounge chair with her legs elevated. She had forgotten how comfortable it was. Her brain must have needed a rest as it wasn't long before she fell asleep. She awoke at twenty past nine and peeked in at her husband who was asleep in his lounge chair. She quickly and quietly got ready for bed. She wanted to give her husband plenty of time to think if he woke up and sat thinking for a while before going to bed. Tomorrow was an exciting day and she needed a good night's sleep to prepare for it. She didn't hear her husband come to bed. He was probably as quiet as she was getting into bed as he likely made sure it was late as he did not want to talk, but ponder what was going on in Meeky's head. He didn't realize he only needed to wait until tomorrow night.

Next morning went as usual. Dominick left at exactly 8:50 a.m. Meeky had stripped the children's beds and washed them. She planned to continue laundry when she returned from shopping. She left her jogging suit on and

170

drove to Goodwill as soon as he was gone. Meeky's shopping trip went better than she thought possible. She found everything she wanted by going to
both Goodwill stores. She ran in to the grocery store and returned in a flash
with two large oranges both the same size. She kept the laundry going until
she had two full baskets of clean items. She added a few white kitchen towels to the dining table linens. She considered folding the children's clothes,
but decided her husband needed just a small sample of what laundry jobs
were. She would leave that load in the dryer, but dry. The next thing she
did was to lay out her Floozy frocks. Nothing needed to be ironed and she
was happy. Her wig needed work so she worked about a half hour getting
it to look like she wanted. Though Meeky realized her scheme was drastic,
she convinced herself it was necessary as no words she could utter would
change a thing with her husband. She found it easier and easier to dismiss
the tiny twinges of guilt that popped in a few times. She told herself it is
like sin. The more you do it, the easier it is to repeat. Meeky was not planning to make up any of the beds. Instead, she was going to take her time
for once. This was her day to enjoy as much as possible. She took a shower,
dried off, put on her panties, a much too-large cupped bra, and stuffed in
two oranges that changed the fit. The mirror was fibbing when she took a
full-length view. She decided she still didn't look like she envisioned Dolly,
but her husband would get the idea. Next she began the task of applying
all her makeup except her face which she would do after she donned her
Floozy top. A classy streetwalker would not have makeup smeared on a
fancy spaghetti strapped top. She had no problem applying the makeup
without streaks. That was a relief as it had to dry and set a few minutes. She
gathered up her nails, lashes, glues, bright red lipstick, and mascara and
put them on the lowered makeup counter in the bathroom where she had
a posh chair that looked brand new because it was almost never used. The
ceiling fan acted as a catalyst in getting her makeup dry and set. It was time
to put on her floozy top and miniskirt. She had checked the fit of them
while in the store; she was glad she hadn't bought a smaller top. Without
the large oranges she had to guess. Appling her makeup was no problem,
but the eyelashes were. She had to get rid of smeared glue after the eye-

lashes were secure and that took her twenty minutes. She barely recognized herself after her face was made up. She walked over to put on her boots and the dog in the doorway bristled and growled at her. She laughed, called his name, and then called him to her to catch her scent. Apparently that had changed with all the makeup and floozy frocks she was wearing because it didn't convince Pamper until she talked more to him and put a handful of dog food in his dish. The bristles on his back were gone and she could pet him without concern. The dog ate and came back to the bedroom door-way and lay down. Meeky was in the room getting the wig pins handy. The dog seemed a bit confused so she let him watch her don the wig as her hair went from a Dorothy Hamill style to a Dolly-do. All seemed well with both the wig and the dog. She used Pampers' name as she occasionally talked to him; he half heartedly gave his tail a half wag as if to say he didn't understand what she is doing, but he would accept her as the real Meeky. Her artificial nails were not the red she wanted, but Goodwill had the right color. She would polish them after she had them glued on her finger nails. It went pretty well. She used her nail dryer on them. It still worked after three years of disuse so her nails dried well.

Meeky looked over the list she would hand Dominick the last instant before darting out the door. The list read: {PM: list numbered 1–8}

1. Pick up one gallon milk for children's breakfast. (Meeky knew that would really disturb him as the camera run had disturbed her.)
2. Make children's beds.
3. Make our bed.
4. Fold and put away children's clothes in dryer. (She knew he had no idea how to fold them or where they went.)
5. Iron tablecloth, two napkins, and your shirt (on doorknob). That was a no-no in Dominick's eyes. Nothing was ever to hang on an inside doorknob of their house. Meeky enjoyed it so much she took it off and re-hung it.

    She said to herself, *Now that was fun, and only the beginning for the evening.* The shirt was hard to iron and Meeky felt she could never make it look good enough for her husband, so she had just left it in the back of the laundry room closet. She thought, *What fun it would be to be a mouse and watch and listen to his reaction.* She thought, *If only I had a camera with sound hidden somewhere. It would be such a great reminder to him.* She decided it was a good idea, but she couldn't do anything about it and dismissed the evil thought. It was moments before a comparable smile left her face.

6. Fix your supper. (You can eat in peace and quiet if you do it before 7:30 p.m. when the kids return.) You have the privilege of fixing whatever you want, except the kid's cereal that they will want in the morning.

7. Run dishwasher after you eat (need cereal bowls for morning).

8. Bathe children and put on clean pajamas (in dryer in laundry room unless you have already folded and put them away). This one would really rile him if he had and maybe even if he hadn't. She decided he could think she was using subtle sarcasm knowing he didn't know how. She added: Allow the children to play at least five minutes in the tub as that is a special time of day for them. It will be a good time for them to tell you all about their stay with their grandparents. After helping them brush teeth, help them with pajamas if they need it (they usually do). Tuck them in with a kiss and read them a story. Clean up bathroom and tub. Had a busy day. Cinderella

Mickey's nails turned out well, *If one likes claws on a woman.* She smiled at that thought. Her next act was to grab her purse out of the closet and make sure her keys were in the outside pocket. She sat her purse at the entry where she would meet Dominick in three minutes. She quickly grabbed the camera, set it on a tripod and took some photos of herself. She decided they just might come in handy some day. Maybe a picture in his den for his birthday would be fun. She quickly put the camera away. Dominick was driving in. She had a moment of a feeling of anxiety mixed with feeling giddy. Dominick walked in and gasped at his first sight of her. He never said a word. She immediately began her rehearsal. She said everything she planned, handed him a neatly folded list and said she needed to go and would be home later. In a flash she was in her car and heading out the driveway. She waved and Dominick just stood there like a statue. He hadn't spoken a word. She drove away feeling a moment of empathy for the man. Again she convinced herself it was the only way she knew to get his attention without a spoken word where there could be no quarrel.

Meeky drove slowly across town. It was rush hour so she stopped at a shopping center that had a nice department store. She had time to kill and the traffic should soon thin. She changed footgear, removed her wig and brushed her hair. After a quick scan of the area she pulled the oranges out of the bra she was wearing. Her spaghetti strap top was going to be pretty roomy, but with a coat over her shoulders she could get by with no problem. She found a pretty lacy bra in her size, bought it, put it on and left for the movies. As Meeky finished her drive to the theater she couldn't help wondering what Dominick was doing and thinking. She was determined to go to the funny movie and enjoy herself. She arrived before many people were lined up for tickets. Meeky bought a big box of buttered popcorn and a cola and waited in a comfortable seat for the movie to start. Time went fast once she got her mind off things at home and on the movie. It was funnier than she had imagined and very cleverly done. Meeky was glad she had thought to bring tissues. A fat lady sitting next to her really had a hearty laugh that was entertaining in itself. She was fun to talk with and the two closely matched the amount of popcorn they ate and colas they drank. After the movie was over they walked out together and stood outside and visited a few minutes while they waited for traffic to clear. Meeky told her what she had done to her husband but made no mention of names. The fat lady thought it was hilarious and would make a funny movie. Meeky was stalling a little as she wanted to make sure her husband had time to get all his chores done. She really didn't know how Dominick was going to react to the events of the evening.

It was 9:45 p.m. when Meeky arrived home. The house was dimly lit. She peeked in on the children and they were in clean pajamas and the bathroom spotless. She was shocked. A folded stack of their clothes was on a chest of drawers. She checked the refrigerator and there was a fresh gallon of milk and the kitchen was neat and clean. The two heaped baskets were empty. Two ironed napkins and a tablecloth were on the buffet. She considered that amazing. Best of all, the shirt was not in sight. She quickly muffled a giggle thinking either he had pitched it or ironed it. The den was dark. Meeky wondered if her husband had even been in it while she was gone. She found it hard to believe that he hadn't at least sucked up his beer there. Meeky was simply amazed at what she had seen after getting home. It seemed like it had to be just a dream; the work her husband did was a first since they were married.

She took off her shoes and quietly peeked in on Dominick. He was snoring like she had never heard him and it wasn't even 10:00 p.m. *He found out what tired is,* she thought, as she quietly reached for her pajamas. Meeky decided she would sleep in the guest bedroom and not disturb her husband. She wanted to have a good talk tomorrow night. Things looked encouraging. She was feeling her schemes had met with some success, but she would have to wait to find out exactly to what extent. Tomorrow would be a long day of suspense for both her husband and her. After getting cleaned up and in her pajamas, Meeky made the decision to leave Dominick a note. She expected the children would have plenty of things to tell her in the morning and she might not have an opportunity to say anything to him. The note said: Home at 9:45 p.m. Didn't want to disturb you. Knew you were tired. Lots to tell you. May have found glass slipper that fits. Let's talk when you get home from work after the children are in bed. Cinderella.

In the morning, Meeky found a note that read: Cinderella, Left at 7:15 a.m. Extra work today. Awaiting your story tonight after kids in bed. Prince Charming.

Meeky had slept until 7:15 a.m. awakening when she heard Dominick leave. That stunned her. She reasoned it must be it was because she had gotten through her schemes and maybe let off more steam than she realized and fell into badly needed bliss. Her children were still not astir. Meeky took the dog out in the backyard and she and the dog ran inside the perimeter of it a few times around. She couldn't leave the children while she walked the dog down the street. Afterwards she made coffee, fed and watered the dog and by then the children were up and telling all about their visit. The four of them and the dog had a good day.

Dominick arrived home an hour early. Meeky was stunned. He behaved like a different man. He asked the children if they would like to play outside in back after he changed his clothes. They looked shocked and after a stare at their father, then their mother, they nodded with big smiles. In a moment Dominick was in his royal blue jogging suit. He called the dog and the children and they all went out the door together. They played until 5:15 p.m. when Dominick came in for his beer and to look at the mail and newspaper. Meeky found it delightful to see the children so happy. They told their mother they had lots of fun. Their faces were all glowing. They were ready to play quiet games in their room until dinner time. After a routine evening for the family Dominick did leave his den and kissed the children goodnight. Meeky had just gotten them tucked in when he came into their bedroom. She was astounded because she hadn't seen him kiss his children since they were young babies. He left the room and retreated back to his den.

The twins almost in unison said, "Daddy kissed us." They were abeam with big smiles.

Little Pricilla said, "Me, too."

Meeky smiled and asked if he did last night and they all responded with a big, "Yes."

That brought another big smile on four faces. It was story time. Meeky kissed her children before she started in case they became sleepy while she read. It was a good thing because Pricilla had fallen asleep and the twins were getting there. Meeky considered the good workout with their father earlier likely contributed as well as a feeling of contentment since he had kissed them the last two nights. Meeky left the room thinking, *Now that is how it should be—instead of a quiet meal at home without the children.* She was still upset about her husband's remark in the dining room two nights earlier. Walking to the den and stepping a foot inside the door, she told her husband the kids were already falling asleep adding that it must be from a good workout in back with their daddy and a nice kiss. He smiled and turned off his television. He motioned her to the sofa telling her it was time for their talk. She nodded and sat on one end of his long sofa. Meeky began the conversation by asking what his early morning job was. He responded by saying he would be brief and to the point because he was anxious to hear what she had to say. Both had a serious demeanor; Meeky nodded.

He told her the first thing he did was to rearrange his secretary's office. A gasp came from Meeky. Dominick explained it was the occupant's choice to have their office set up as they preferred and he stuck his neck out in changing it. Dominick told Meeky he knew his secretary would be livid when she came in at 8:00 a.m. and found it was changed, and she was.

Her first words were, "How dare anybody do this?"

Dominick said she spun around and accused him of doing it and he immediately admitted he did. He had moved her desk near the far left wall and that was what she protested most. Meeky gasped again. She was not going to interrupt him, only listen to everything he said, but the gasps seemed to just happen.

Her husband next told her that his secretary rushed towards him as he sat at his desk and screamed," I quit."

He said he responded calmly with," Each to his own."

Meeky found herself sitting near the edge of her seat instead of back with her elbow resting on the sofa arm. He said she stormed out of his office and began gathering up her personal belongings. Drawers were being jerked open and slammed shut. She marched out of her office with a full shopping bag on one shoulder and her purse strap on the other.

She stopped in front of his office, pointed her finger at him and yelled," You will never find a secretary as good I am."

He said he told her he already knew one who would make her look like she came to the office for vacation.

He pointed at his wife and Meeky chuckled as she listened in awe. He told Meeky everyone in the row of offices all down the hall on both sides heard her throwing her tantrum and stomping down the hall to the exit door. Of course they all watched her, too. She was not looking left or right.

He said except for the noise his secretary was making, all the offices were quiet. They knew his secretary had quit. Dominick told his wife that as soon as his secretary left, all the employees gathered in the hall, walked in his office and clapped their hands and were ready to leave when he stopped them asking how they felt about her. He said they all felt she had a superior attitude toward the other employees and they didn't like her. They saw her appearance as ridiculous and only tolerated her. They knew she was single and needed work and seemed good at her job.

Dominick said he thanked them all for their opinions and said as long as she was seeking work where there was a dress code he would recommend her. The employees agreed as she started out more modestly dressed but gradually became bolder.

Meeky's husband explained it is a legal hassle and expensive to establish a dress code after the fact so that was why it hadn't been done. He said in the past it hasn't been needed in this type of work. He then dismissed the crowd to return to work.

He told Meeky he was relieved she was gone as her presence reflected poorly on the whole place. Meeky was relieved. He said it was Meeky who gave him the incentive to do what he should have done long ago. With a big smile Meeky thanked him.

He said he was at the end of his story and it was her turn. What Meeky just heard was a big revelation and her mind was whirling. She sat quietly for a moment staring into space like she had just turned off a movie. She felt some resentment because her husband had never before told her anything about his secretary's appearance and nothing about the dress code problem. She wondered what else had he kept from her. Before she started telling her story she decided that she would be very open to her husband and reveal all the emotions she experienced while living with him.

Meeky sat back on the sofa and took a good half hour of steady talk to tell Dominick everything about her last two days which was brought on after meeting his Floozy secretary. That was her first verbal reference about how she saw his secretary. She covered all the emotions she has felt the last three years and how tired she was all the time from working so hard. She minced no words and spared none. Dominick listened to her every word. She had no hesitation in telling him that she knew words expressed to him would be ignored and this was his last chance to hear what she was saying and take action to change many things or she and the children would soon leave along with half of their money and material possessions.

He had never heard her talk like that and he knew it was to be taken seriously. Meeky spared no words in how she felt about his lack of interaction or help with the children. She said based on the past she felt he wouldn't even mind if they were gone. She began to cry and pulled a tissue from her apron pocket. Dominick got up out of his chair and sat beside her sort of fidgeting with his hands and not looking directly at her while he talked.

He told her she had given him good cause to do a lot of thinking. He revealed he just had not realized how he had treated her because he was not tuned in to what was happening in the home. He saw household matters and rearing the children as her duties as a wife and mother. He said he truly believed he had every right to expect the house to be a quiet and clean place of his refuge because he brought in a good income. He volunteered he hadn't considered that she had no escape from her workplace. He said in his selfishness he hadn't considered all the work she had to do to keep the house clean and all the other daily demands she had to meet. He admitted after the one evening of work he did around the house it opened his eyes. He told her he couldn't wait to get to bed after he was done and he never went into the den all evening. Ever since he has wondered how she could possibly accomplish all she did daily. Meeky had gone through her tissues. He reached into his pocket and pulled out a well ironed neatly folded handkerchief and handed it to her, then put his arm around her. Meeky didn't move except to blow her nose. Suddenly she blurted out that she was giving him credit for being smarter than he really was. Dominick flinched. After a few seconds he looked her in the face and said he just realized how blind self-centered people like himself are to other's needs. Meeky only nodded and gave a quick glimpse at his face.

He said, "That is in the past and don't let it concern you anymore."

Dominick tried to cheer his wife up a little and told her he knew she was very bright, but didn't know she had such talent and imagination to dream up and pull off the schemes she did. He said he deserved what she had done and admitted it really threw him into a shocked state of being and he realized what seeing his secretary must have done to her. He reached in his other pocket and handed his wife a neatly folded stack of ten, one-hundred dollar bills. He immediately told her he wanted her to have Saturdays off after he had his hair and nails done. He said the money was for her to replace badly needed clothes that fit. He told her he wanted to see her in sharp dressy jeans, tops and comfortable classy shoes around the house. He wanted her to get rid of the plastic apron, shoes, and muumuus. Meeky said in a louder voice than usual and more adamantly that it would be easy if she didn't have to shampoo the dog and do the gardening and mop floors every day. He said he would take care of all that by hiring a good gardener and in good weather he would shampoo the dog and other times take him in for a shampoo and clip. Also, he would hire a cleaning crew to come in every Saturday, so other than an occasional spill, Meeky wouldn't need to mop. He added that he would take the children outside after dinner and play with them and the dog for an hour when weather permitted. He said he would interact with the children much more than he had and they would get their nightly kiss from their daddy from now on.

Meeky was barely able to believe it, but was willing to have him give it a try and she told him so. He husband looked a bit surprised, but continued on by relating the changes he was willing to make. Dominick told Meeky she would not have to get up at 5:30 a.m. in the morning anymore, and that 7:00 a.m. should work fine. If she wanted to run the dog in good weather which she said she enjoyed, he would get up, make coffee and set up the breakfast bowls and cereal for the children and he would be happy with just a muffin and coffee for breakfast. It could be one from the bakery just two blocks from the house. He said she didn't have to spend a long while fixing breakfast anymore. The children like cereal so they would likely be happy with that. Dominick said there would be time to have their coffee and muffin together before the children were up. He would have time to get ready for work and a little time for the children before he left. It sounded wonderful to Meeky.

Everything he promised Meeky is being fulfilled. Meeky now has time to enjoy the children more and their nice home. Saturdays off are wonderful. She feels like a fortunate human being again and likes her lifestyle. Dominick is much more social with her and the children. The entire atmosphere has changed in the household. The children and parents are much happier people. The name Cinderella is never used anymore. Meeky and Dominick have made some wonderful friends from the church. The couples and their children camp out together and do all sorts of fun things socially. That was never done before.

The pastor's daughter is Dominick's secretary and she is very efficient and well liked by all the employees. If Meeky and Dominick want a night out without the children another daughter babysits and the children love her. Meeky has no desire to work outside the home anymore. She is very contented with the life she is living. Dominick said he has never been happier. Life is good because of determination to make it so. Many negatives have been overcome. Change isn't easy for Dominick, but he realizes what he has and his intention to overcome is prevailing. He gives his wife credit for bringing him to his senses and sticking with him in giving him a chance to prove himself. Dominick still is a type-A personality, but long ago he made a conscious effort to modify his behavior. He thinks as does Meeky, *like sin, the more you do it the easier it becomes.*

Chapter 27

Mama's Latter Years

Mama loved her years at the lake home until Daddy became ill and life became very hectic for her. Daddy took enough care that professional people in the health field could not believe she had done it alone in their home.

After Daddy died Mama could not deal with the snow and it made no sense for her to have to do it. She made the decision to move out west where there she had family. She moved into a small complex of gated and safe townhouses where many older people lived. Everyone sort of watched over each other. My sister had lost her husband and she moved out west into one of the townhouses where she and Mama were in close proximity. At eighty-two, Mama was capable of caring for herself, but in a few years her eyesight was failing due to macular degeneration. She could no longer drive so she went grocery shopping and other places with Oleta. They had lots of fun times together. Both used their good sense of humor and enjoyed each other.

Six years after living in the townhouses, Oleta wanted to move to another western state and Mama needed to move to stay near her daughter so she and Oleta bought homes just across the street from each other. It was in that town where Oleta met the man she married after being widowed. After this marriage, Oleta moved across town in the house her husband owned. Her daughter and husband lived in the house Oleta owned until it sold. Mother became accustomed to her new home and a new church quickly. She was able to tend to all her needs, except driving. She often walked to the drug store and a small grocery store while using her red and white cane in crossing the street.

After living seven years in that town, Oleta wanted to move back to the town she and Mama had left. Her husband was willing so Mama sold her home and went back to her townhouse in the other state as it had not sold. Mama was now ninety years of age.

Her eyesight became so poor after a year or so she finally had to give up her independence as she could no longer live alone. Oleta and her husband invited her to move in with them. Mama was alert and able to do much for herself. Oleta washed her laundry and Mama folded and put her things away. She remained alert, and usually kept her sense of humor, but was capable of speaking her mind as well.

She still watched programs on television she was familiar with. Giving up her independence was a big adjustment for Mama. Both families had adjustments to make. It wasn't always easy for either of them. I remember visiting there and Mama repeating by memory the poem of "Abu Ben Adam" she learned as a young girl. After a few years in that home, Oleta wanted to move to Arkansas where our sister, Charlene and her husband lived. Oleta and her husband sold their home and moved to Arkansas taking Mama with them. Once again, Mama became accustomed to another home. By then, she was nearly blind, but she managed quite well. Unfortunately, after a while in that home Mama fell and broke her hip. She was almost ninety-five, but she was home from the hospital in a week following surgery. She faithfully did her exercises and her doctor was amazed at her progress. She recovered well. She had grit and determination above many people I have known. Beside her vision deficit, her hearing continued to fail. Within a year after he hip surgery there was almost nothing she could do for entertainment. Going to church no longer made sense. Living had become bleak for her.

Mama became restless and often paced with her walker. She would get tired and want to go to bed. She understandably became confused between night and day. Her sight was so poor she couldn't really tell the time of day by the outside light that barely sifted through the windows. Mama had little appetite and even her favorite foods so longer appealed to her. She was no longer interested in eating to live. Another time when she was pacing, she fell and broke her other hip. She was ninety-six. The doctor said there was nothing he could do for her other than help keep her comfortable.

Mama was put in bed and because moving was so painful she couldn't do it or stand someone else moving her.

She passed away in a few days. Mama was ready for a better life. She was very confident that is what she had to anticipate. She had strong faith in God and believed His promises. I believe Mama saw life as a supreme God-given gift to be cherished with an obligation to live life responsibly. We children feel she did. We greatly loved our mother. We found great comfort in knowing that Mama left her misery behind knowing she would be in her Heavenly home. It would be a great adventure for her that would last in bliss forever. She knew she would be with loved ones when she arrived. She expected to one day have more of them with her. When the time came, Mama knew she could just enjoy her children with no work in caring for them or no concerns. It will be good to see her again healthy and happy beyond what we can ever imagine with our finite minds.

Chapter 28

Summary

I have felt we children were at a disadvantage when we started high school as we came from a rural area and attended rural school through the eighth grade. We didn't know people in our class or school, except for Oleta who knew two in her grade. We were minorities in rural school. We lived in a tiny crowded house and lived rather primitively even when we three started high school. Those were reasons that caused us to feel a bit inferior. Attending a new large school in town was somewhat intimidating. Many of the students had known each other from the time they began school. We soon found that fitting in was not difficult. We fit in better than in rural school because very few were Mennonites so we had a better sense of belonging. We did well in school scholastically and found friends who did that as well. In time we had lots of friends and were well liked by all the teachers, superintendent and principal.

Oleta and I were both asked by our English teacher to be librarians so we did that for a few years. We played saxophones in the band and were in some of the school plays. When we were available on days when was no school, we babysat and did other jobs for people in our neighborhood on Saturdays. That gave us a little money to buy the latest styles in shoes and clothing once in a while. In summer Oleta and I both worked for people in town; we saved up what seemed like a lot of money to us and bought school clothes when we amassed enough to buy items special to us. Because Mama was teaching school, she needed help with household duties, garden work, and in preparing foods for canning.

I was going to be seventeen when I graduated. We were not allowed to date until we were sixteen. I was at some disadvantage as I was graduating a little younger than most of the others in my grade. I had a girlfriend who liked roller skating and who often asked me to stay overnight with her. Her aunt took us skating at the local rink where I learned how to skate very quickly. We had so much fun. It was a popular entertainment for high school kids but none of my sisters were interested in it. I met a fellow from another school who was a very good skater and did the fancy skating. He saw my girlfriend and me skate to the circle waltz and do other skate dancing and asked me to skate with him; we skated well together. Eventually we started dating. My girlfriend was dating too. We both married the men we were dating. My girlfriend married soon after graduation from high school. I went on to nursing school so marriage came later for me. When I was in my senior year of high school, another girlfriend of mine and I started the Future Nurses Club. The girls who attended all became nurses.

All of us children in the family liked high school once we became acquainted with others. We enjoyed being in band and other extracurricular activities. We had relatives on my father's side from the big city of Detroit who were into dancing. Both parents were fabulous dancers and their daughter tap danced. I was most intrigued with it as dancing always looked like fun to me. When they came to visit us they brought movies of themselves in dance competition and of their daughter performing in beautiful dresses. I wanted to take lessons but there were none available. My parents weren't keen on the idea. I did go to the senior prom with the man I married. He was a good dancer.

A few years after I married, my farmer-husband a group of us in the community got together and learned how to do ballroom dancing and square dancing. We had lots of fun. We did this in the winter months when the men couldn't farm. In the summer we all had plenty of work to keep us busy. We all were fairly close in age and had young families. The women did gardening and what farmer's wives do. Getting all six of the little ones in our family ready for church took preparation ahead of time. After the children were done with breakfast and the dishes done up, I fixed what we would have for our noon meal that I baked in the oven on low while we were gone. If we didn't eat early enough some of the little ones would fall asleep before they ate or be ready for naps. I had no desire to prepare food again for the little ones later after getting the dishes done and the kitchen back in order following Sunday dinner.

After getting the Sunday meal ready, it was time to load the diaper bag, make beds, help with tooth brushing, and washing up little children who had been bathed the night prior. Then I laid out clothes for the children and dressed the ones who couldn't do it on their own, and helped some of the others. Heads of hair to brush and comb followed. They all needed quiet play so they didn't get their clothes or hair looking disheveled playing. Television took care of that while I dressed for church. Their daddy finished milking cows, came in and cleaned up and dressed for church while I set the table and gathered up hats, coats, and gloves for myself and the little girls. The last thing was to get shoes on everybody before we walked out the door for our drive to church and Sunday school. More than once I checked to see if I had remembered to remove my apron.

Several years later we moved from the Breckenridge area to the Traverse City area in northern Michigan. My husband was giving up farming to get into construction with a fellow who lived there. We felt a bigger school would offer more to bright kids who would likely want to go to college. Two of them were in high school. Many years after attending nursing school, being married and having six children, I went to work outside the home after all our six children were in school.

I worked in the mental health field in direct care of patients at our local psychiatric hospital in the town of Traverse City near where we lived. Part of the time I carried a full load of classes each semester from the local college to pick up classes I needed to further my formal education. At first going back to college was scary but I did well. Before I went to work outside the home, we built a large five bedroom home on the bay of Lake Michigan. I had designed it and after it was built I did all the finish work like papering, staining, painting, and all that was necessary to complete it inside and out. I did the landscaping as well. We were asked to have it featured in the local annual tour of homes for one season and accepted. With seven people living in it we still kept it looking neat and clean. We had to be organized for that to happen.

After I started working out of the home I had all I could handle to keep up with everything. A day off from the hospital was not a day off for me.

It meant a chance to do laundry, and some thorough cleaning, a little gardening, and sometimes some extra baking, cooking, and studying. At the hospital where I started working, all personnel in the service of direct care were required to take many classes. I greatly enjoyed them.

I found my work very interesting and rewarding and grew close to many of the patients. They lead such pathetic and seemingly useless lives; it was sad to see. Some were young while many had been in the institution for years and had grown old there. They were not stupid by any means. Many were very clever but it was nearly impossible to get any of them to smile. There were a few who laughed to themselves when nobody was nearby. Personal hygiene meant a constant struggle to get most of them to take care of themselves. Many times we who tended to their care had to help them or do much of it for them. When we were hired we each were requested to select a patient from the ward we worked and spend extra time and effort with one of them. Part of our class assignment was to keep records of all the conversations and the demeanor of the patient. I chose a man who had long resided there with a diagnosis of being a paranoid schizophrenic. The doctor and instructor were very reluctant as he was around sixty-two and had been in the hospital for years. They felt strongly that he was a poor candidate. I agreed if I had no success with him that I would start over with another patient. I told them I really wanted to see if I could bring about any changes in the man.

Some of my co-workers kidded me saying, "So you think you are going to cure him, huh?" Then they would laugh and maybe give me a pat on the shoulder and walk away.

My patient displayed many of the typical characteristics of a person of that diagnosis which were indifference, withdrawal from others, hallucinations and delusions of persecution, but not of grandeur as some do. He was going to be a real challenge. I told him I wanted to work with him and help life get better for him. He sat politely and said nothing. I had seen him standing alone every day at the far end of a very long hall that led from the dayroom where some sat and watched television. I never saw him interact with anyone. He was one of the patients who kept himself neatly

188

shaven, hair neatly combed and clean. Somehow, I saw him as having more potential for recovery than many on the ward. One patient who wore a tie everyday spilled his meal on it as well as on his suit coat. He wore the same tie day after day unless I could get him to wash it and wear a different one. Whenever I mentioned his tie was dirty, he gave it a quick glance, brushed his hand over it and said it was okay. I told him it wasn't. I asked him to go get a free one at the canteen area. He turned me in by letter to the head doctor of the hospital. The doctor called me saying he had a complaint about me from a patient. My heart felt like it went from my chest to my throat for a moment. He congratulated me, telling me to keep up the good work. He said more employees need to do the same. The man had outdoor privileges and often walked downtown. His general appearance was a poor reflection of the hospital. It was obvious to others in town that he came from the psychiatric hospital. The doctor related he had seen him there more than once and was happy I was paying attention to the patient's appearance. One never knew what a patient might do to try to eliminate someone who disturbed them and I often did.

I had no idea if the man I was working intensely with would show hostility toward me but it would not have surprised me. I began speaking to him by name every morning I came on duty. He gave a slight nod, but never made eye contact. He was always standing in front of the barred window not far from the door I used for entry to the ward. I might make a comment about it being a beautiful day and add that he might wish to take a nice long walk outside during the day. He said nothing and continued to just stare ahead. Only a very careful slow start was going to allow me to peel off his shell and get inside his head. I knew not to even pat his shoulder or hand after our conversation ended. I never touched him or he me. I started our first sessions by holding them for a few minutes. In the beginning I asked him why he was here. With no eye contact, he said he has a blood clot on the brain. I asked him how long he had been in the hospital and his answer was like the other one as very inappropriate.

I knew not to bring it up again. I already knew what his chart revealed, and knew the answers. I wanted him to deal with reality. He was married and once in every few months his wife made a long trip to come and see him. I asked about her. All I learned from him was that she worked. Since she had stayed married to him all the years he was gone, I knew she had to work outside the home. It opened a door so I could ask him where he had worked. He gave a brief response that it was in a car manufacturing plant. After he became a little comfortable with me, I got more of a response from him. He finally told me what his specific job was. Many weeks later I got him to go with me for the ward mail as we had a large underground tunnel to traverse. He said he would. I was delighted. That was a giant step for him and encouraging to me. I handed him the mail basket when we arrived at the first metal gate that I needed to unlock and lock. He took the basket. I asked if he would keep it as I had more gates to unlock and lock. He nodded and I thanked him. He was polite, but quiet. I didn't prod him with questions much as I was in a vulnerable spot with only the two of us. I purposely gave him the idea I felt safer having him with me. I could sense a slight glimmer of pride in his slight stature change. It was like he was on the lookout for me as my security guard. He knew some patients were dangerous. Usually they didn't have ground privileges. If so, it would not be a foreseen risk if there were a sudden flare up with one of them.

There was an incident where one from a violent ward had earned a good behavior award to let him out for a short time to test him. He had been on a locked ward for a long while. I worked the ward next door. It was an unlocked ward. I had gone down a hall around a corner where nobody was in sight. He had just walked in from the outside and I was shocked to see him there. He and I were on the same side of a very solid steel door that separated us from everyone else. I asked him what he was doing on our ward and he told me he came over to kiss me. It sent a chill straight through me. He was a big young fellow and it alarmed me. I told him I had a big family at home and needed my job and I would be fired for such a thing. He knew who I was as there were occasions when I needed to go to the ward he was on for a medication we didn't have on my ward next door. I never went without calling ahead to say I needed some of the employed men to meet me at the door. He was always with them and always ogled me. I told him to leave as he would be in trouble. I knew if he took enough chance to walk in on our ward to try to kiss me he might want to see me still working at the hospital. Opening the heavy steel door hoping to get on the other side of it where I could more likely be heard if I had to yell for help could not have happened soon enough. He had stood between me and it. When I repeated about moving out the door he moved enough so I could reach the steel door. It took me only a moment to get back to the office and call his ward and report him. He was back under lock and key in a hurry.

I always tried to be cautious around the patients as it was foolish not to be alert. I didn't often feel afraid. I decided any chance of riling my special patient could jeopardize my safety. I had been in some precarious circumstances on the training ward before being assigned this all male ward of lesser aggressive patients. After he held the basket and I placed the mail in it I suggested another route where we could walk outside. I asked if he would carry the basket.

He nodded and said, "Okay."

We strolled along in the beautiful weather. There were other people on the beautiful grounds; most of them were patients. Sometimes I stopped and said a little to them. I think he felt more like a real human when he was outside with me. That was my purpose in getting him out and about in a somewhat more normal environment. I got him talking a little, but he didn't volunteer anything. He just answered my questions of little consequence. I kept it as small talk in an attempt to make him gradually more comfortable. It seemed to be working.

When I was having the next day off I always told him ahead of time. I told him I would see him tomorrow at 10:30 a.m. when I was planning to be back. I kept our meetings at the same time to give him confidence in me. Our getting the mail together became routine. He began to just automatically hold his hand out for the basket. That was a huge change. I was thrilled.

After a few weeks of meeting with him I asked him if he would like to leave the hospital for good. He said he didn't know. I asked him to take his time and think on it for a few days. He had become very comfortable there at the hospital with no responsibility except to keep himself neat and clean. I knew it would be a huge change and very frightening for him. Many patients become institutionalized and don't want to leave and deal with the real world. There was no way I could be sure of his response.

He was making some eye contact with me by now. I mentioned I appreciated him always looking neat and clean; he nodded in appreciation. I never saw him smile, but he was always pleasant when with me. He seemed somewhat relaxed this day so it seemed the perfect day to ask him again about his feeling about leaving. He said he would be willing to try it. What a joy it was to hear him say these words. I told him I had confidence in him that he would soon be out and never be back. He remained quiet and sat with a very serious look on his face. I told him in a few days we could talk with the doctor about it. He nodded very slightly.

We had a new crisis unit opening and I was asked to be part of the team. It sounded like a perfect spot for me. The idea was not to keep a patient over two weeks with more intense therapy so they would not become comfortable in settling in at the hospital and end up there while they became institutionalized. As soon as I knew I would be part of the staff I gave my special patient all the warning time I had before I left. I never met with him and the doctor as I was transferred to the new unit very soon. I told him I would not forget him and I hoped to see him out on the grounds, and then added that better than that I expected to soon hear he had been discharged.

In a few weeks he was discharged from the hospital, and amazingly, after many years there he went back to work. I don't know that any patient who was ever in this hospital as long as he was ever released to outside living back in the family. I did not let negativity of others thwart me. I was the new one at the hospital and was tempted to believe they knew him better than I, but I did not yield to that .He had been there at his place of work long enough that he had retirement income due him in a short time. He died of a heart attack not long after he went back to work which I am sure it was stressful for him. I never heard if he lived long enough that his wife could collect on his retirement but she deserved it. At least her husband died with more dignity by leaving the hospital and going back to work.

I tell this story because I saw two people overcome something that was a huge obstacle. It appears that one just needed a little intervention to put him back on track. Maybe his engine wasn't quite up to its peak condition, but it was forging onward. He needed encouragement. As for his wife, she did what she needed to do financially. She remained married to her ill husband for many years. There had to have been some big sacrifices made on her part. Dealing with a paranoid mate had to be difficult. Having to finally place him in a psychiatric hospital must have been a painful decision.

I am glad I went that extra mile for my patient. I don't know of a person at the hospital who thought the man would ever leave. Not one person ever said a word to me about my part in the man's discharge as their pride kept them from it. None wanted to eat crow. How sad they saw it that way; I wasn't doing it for compliments. It never entered my mind. It is only in retrospect as I write this that I realize that was the way it went. My patient didn't need much of a nudge and that was all he got from me, but it made a difference. It is a truth that even seemingly insurmountable adversities can be overcome. The results may not always be exactly as hoped, but they will likely be as intended. I often wondered if many of the patients were possessed by evil spirits. There were a very few cases where exorcisms were performed and were successful. Maybe there should have been many.

About two years after his discharge from the hospital it began a phase out process. I had worked there several years, but was still among the newer employees. At the start of closing the hospital over two hundred of us out of around three thousand employees were given pink slips. We were all done working there. It was a state hospital and the order of those leaving was based only on years of service with the state of Michigan. Many people told me they not want me to leave, but they had no choice. I told them I hated to leave just as much. It really seemed my niche. The crisis intervention unit closed for lack of funds. Its purpose was great, but had only just nicely gotten functioning well when it had to close. Not long after that our family moved out west from Michigan. My husband and his construction partner found that since they were non-union their expensive machinery was being damaged with slashed tires, sugar in the gas tanks, and other vandalism. The winters were cold and we desired to be where there was work building houses and commercial buildings year round.

It may not have been where we were supposed to be as things just didn't work out well. Both my husband and I and his partner and wife broke up while we were out there. All four of us ended in divorce. I had established a clothing store right after we moved there. After nine years I sold it and moved back to Traverse City. All our children had returned in pursuit of colleges they wanted to attend in Michigan and for various other reasons. I had a lease I could not break and was stuck out west longer than the others.

Life was very different for me. I finally sold my business and returned to Michigan. I eventually met a man in Traverse City who had a cabin near the area and a home in southern Michigan. He had lost his wife and said he had no plans to remarry. After some time dating, however, we did plan to marry. About two weeks before our wedding date he was stricken with a serious stroke. His doctor was a close friend of his and was greatly surprised. It stunned me as he was such a lively person. My fiancé looked and acted the picture of health. He never knew a stranger and had a seemingly endless list of friends and saw many fairly frequently. He was only sixty three when he was stricken. Instead of a wedding, my kids and I attended a huge funeral almost on the day we were to marry. His adult children and mine were planning on standing up with us at the wedding. They greatly liked him. My kids were about as numb with shock as I. Life for me was soon to go through another big change. The day he was stricken he planned to get me set up where I would never have any financial concerns but it never happened. I was left in a financial mess with no job. He had asked me to quit work and help him redo his Florida home to my liking and the lake home he had recently purchased. We were to spend winters in a home he had in Florida and Michigan on the lake home in the warm weather and fall. We had recently finished both houses.

For many years after my husband and I ended our marriage, I remained single. I was never able to get back in the mental health field as there were no psychiatric hospitals where I lived so I worked in home nursing care and other fields. Eventually I remarried.

After getting education beyond high school in their chosen fields, all my sisters married and had families. My brother married while in college, and he and his wife had four children. Our only brother and the baby of the family left this world just days before his sixty-third birthday. He had just had some heart correction surgery done and it was very successful. At that time the doctors discovered he had enlarged lymph nodes in his lower neck area and advised he have them checked soon. He did and it was found he had lung and liver cancer and was given six weeks to live. The doctors were right. Losing him was a very sad time in our lives. Mama lived to see her only son and baby of the family pass away. We sisters all greatly miss him. He was a fun and interesting man.

My sisters are all retired now and we see each other occasionally, but communicate by computer or telephone. Florida, Michigan and Arkansas are where we now are scattered and reside. We love each other. It is fun to think of the many good times we have had together. Playing school may have been one of the highlights of our growing up years together as it was the time when we all played together more at the same time. We surely did spend much time together in very close quarters. It was barely possible not to be in someone's face when we were almost shoulder to shoulder.

It is interesting that even when all share the same nest that siblings can be so different. People react differently to the same situation, be it sad, funny or scary. We have all kept our sense of humor. I am still considered the busy one. It is just who I am and always expect to be.

I mention in this book that my mother called me that from when a baby and she did not necessarily mean it as wildly complimentary. It would not surprise me if my sisters still see me as sort of a rascal which is what my mother may have been thinking. She did say I didn't stay in one place long and I still don't. Writing this book has kept me on my seat in one spot longer than most things I have done.

There are many things of much interest to me. Redoing houses has been fun for me the past several years. I love life. Some people see their cup as half full and some as half empty. Some see a rainy day as gloomy and can barely tolerate it until the sun shines again. Others see it as wonderful when the dust settles and is out of the air we breathe and when plants get their badly needed water and everything seems fresh and clean. It makes a great difference on what one's focus is. Nobody likes attending a pity-party except the one giving it. It is so much more pleasant for all concerned to get over one's self and focus on making life better for others. It has therapeutic value for the giver and receiver. Living under God's principles works so much better. It is He who we can rely upon to give us wisdom and blessings when we view a coin from one side, but that really does always have two sides.

My adult children are all in the health field except one who is a college graduate and works as a systems analyst. The others range from registered nurses to an anesthetist, a physician, dental hygienist and one who counsels those with personal need. They are all humble, kind people and are successful in their work as are their spouses. They are all wonderful parents. One family has two in college. Another family has one who has graduated with his PhD and does research in the laser field pertaining to health matters. One more family has a son who has graduated with an engineering degree and has training in robotics. Some pertains to prosthetics. They have another son in college. Also, they have taken in a young man from a foreign country and treat him like a son and are helping him financially with college. His father deserted the family and his mother, who he greatly loved, recently passed away. The other two families have children who aren't old enough for college, but look like good candidates. I have been blessed with the large family I always wanted and could never have hoped to have a better one. I am very blessed.

Please understand that it is a Biblical principle that dwelling on your fears brings them upon you. Stepping out in faith to overcome or to attain good goals is the way to succeed. It takes unwavering intention on your part to do it. Intention becomes etched in one's psyche. It is a motivational force and it brings action. Anything worthwhile is not easy, but the results are well worth the effort. It makes life meaningful and shows one has appreciation for their God-given gift of their very life. Living it responsibly is everyone's duty. Remember that God has a purpose for each person and it just may be that when one feels drawn to a certain work, place or person that it is what God has planned for you. Heed it. The closer you grow to God the more wisdom, peace and joy, plus many more blessings come into your life. I can vouch for that. I only regret that I hadn't gotten closer much sooner.

As for the rearing of children, some people are unaware that they damn them by the words they speak to them. Children need to hear positive Godly things come from parent's mouths. Thoughts need to be guarded just as one's words as both are powerful. They can come from Satan as well as God. Choose carefully as Satan is always ready to corrupt. Don't doubt it for a minute. Look what is happening in this world and has for centuries. If it is not good it is not from God but from Satan. Children learn corruption as quickly as they learn to live as God would have them. Parents are responsible for what their children learn. Satan does not want them to be God's children. He wants them for himself from very early in life. He uses every opportunity to accomplish this. Even in what is considered good families, but lukewarm parents that don't have a God-centered home, the children are very vulnerable to Satan's attacks and are likely to get caught up in his snares. Children do live what they learn. They learn apathy when it is the attitude of parents concerning God. Rearing children is a big responsibility. There is much more to it than meeting their physical needs. A good place to start is praying for them and lovingly talking to them even before they are born.

As I was finishing this book, I learned that my granddaughter who has been spending her second year in college has called it quits mid-year. Until I learned the reason I just could not imagine such a thing in her case. It just was not the stuff she was made of to be a quitter. This girl was a nearly straight A student all through school from the beginning. Every teacher she ever had saw her as the epitome of the perfect student not only scholastically, but in her relationships with others. She has been an outstanding athlete and finally had to choose a sport for focus. Basketball was her choice. She played the position of point guard for years as it demanded a leader and one who well understood the game. She performed exceptionally well from the sixth grade. One coach gave her private lessons as he saw an outstanding player. She was even asked to teach upper classmen some fine points of shooting the ball into the basket. She had built up her muscles and could run like a deer. Her brother chided that he didn't need to protect her from the bad guys as she was perfectly capable on her own. My granddaughter is a most unselfish player, but a dedicated team player. During the summer of her junior year when my granddaughter would normally be attending summer camp with players from many schools, she was not able to be there until the season was nearly over. It was a critical time for her as she would be a senior in high school and when scouts select those they want to play for a given college. She had developed a serious problem with one leg that affected the groin area. She kept her mouth shut about it until she could barely move her leg forward. Her coach noticed she was not moving one leg as far forward as the other. Soon doctors were involved and she was finally sent a great distance to the university hospital in Ann Arbor where they suspected bone cancer as did her mother, a registered nurse who works in oncology. She went in for surgery and that is not what they found, but tried to correct the problem. It appeared that she was not going to play basketball in college.

After years of consistent practice she had never considered that possibility. My granddaughter was on crutches much of the summer. One day while lying on the bed she noticed her leg didn't hurt and felt she would be able to move her leg in ways she hadn't been able for months. Though the doctors told her not to do it, she tried and was successful. She got up, left her crutches behind and walked pain-free down an open stairway and across the house, then ran and did all sorts of exercises pain-free. Hours before she could not do any of what she did. When her mother arrived home from work she stood at the door with no crutches and was crying and jumping up and down and saying it seemed a had a miracle. Her mother soon agreed that had to be the case. The tears flowed from them both. Soon her father was home from work. They both met him at the door crying. He was alarmed. For reasons he didn't understand he felt a strong urge to stop and pick up floating balloons on his way home. Though it made no sense he did it. As soon as his daughter showed him what she could do with no crutches and no pain, he turned on his heel walked to his car and brought back the balloons to his daughter. He agreed it was a miracle.

My daughter called her daughter's main doctor the next day saying he would likely not believe it but her daughter was suddenly healed Her doctor insisted she be seen at her scheduled appointment just a few days away. Upon thoroughly examining her leg the doctors could find nothing wrong and they could not explain it scientifically. The media was after her for interviews. There were articles in newspapers and word spread to other schools that played against her school. She received a great deal of cards and letters from them and all around the community. She was well known. As she was encouraged to do so, she gave talks of inspiration to other students.

My granddaughter went to camp for the few days that were left. She played well with no problem. Scouts had watched her play even before high school. She had a reputation that was outstanding. Because of her overall performance in sports and scholastic achievement she was offered an $80,000 scholarship from a college she chose. She also was awarded another $2000 local scholarship.

She graduated with some six hundred others in her class. She was told the college she selected needed a point guard and good team leader. It appeared they felt she was that person. She had earned that position where leadership and skill was greatly needed. It seemed perfect to her. In order to keep her scholarship with the college she was to maintain a near perfect average grade scholastically, and she did, even though she suffered a broken nose and had to have surgery and be out of school a week of her first year of college. Her coach was shocked when she came to class with eyes nearly swollen shut and a black and blue face. It was then he said she needed to be seen by a doctor and she learned from the doctor that she needed surgery.

During her first year and half of college her coach of twenty-five years of experience told her she was the best leader he ever had. He told her she understood basketball better than any player he had ever coached. She had the best record of baskets of her team mates and made few mistakes. She was known for that. He didn't spare his compliments to her in the very beginning of the first year, but let others get away with terrible errors and would come down on her hard and bench her for the game when he didn't like a play she made.

Strangely, she soon barely got off the bench when playing other schools. That was a new experience for her and when she did she would be back in minutes. She didn't understand. She consulted with the coach nearly every Friday asking what was wrong. He would praise her and never explain a thing to help her know what he wanted. It was shattering her confidence. There were times during a game where she never played that the coach admitted to all the team he just didn't know what tactic to use to beat the other team. My granddaughter, like a loyal teammate most politely made suggestions that might work as the team and coach gathered for a moment of problem solving or whatever the coach deemed necessary. He used my Granddaughter's advice and it worked every time and she went back to sit on the bench.

Another time he pulled her back off the floor to the bench as he was unhappy with a play she made. Seeking constructive criticism once again, she asked him what he would have done under the circumstances and he told her he didn't know and walked away. That is the sort of thing she graciously endured until she could no longer see any point.

Her dream was to become a coach after college and teach players to truly understand the game and learn how to play well. The longest playing time for her in a game was thirteen minutes. Her parents drove a great distance to see the game. She may have mentioned they were coming and he decided to let her play more. Some time before attending the game her mother spoke with the coach for forty-five minutes and it seemed a healthy worthwhile conversation. She explained her daughter wanted his constructive criticism, but was unable to learn what he wanted and her confidence

Phyllis Bigelow

was being shattered. She saw others make mistakes and get gentle explanation from him that was beneficial in making them better players. She was becoming confused about what she was part of. After the game her parents watched him compliment their daughter greatly on her play in that game. The next day they had another game and she never left the bench. After the game the coach announced to the team that he owed my granddaughter and one other girl an apology that they didn't get to play. The coach's daughter was a first string freshman and played point guard this second year my granddaughter was on the team. My granddaughter almost never got to play that position as another freshman did her first year and obviously lacked my granddaughter's understanding and skills. As mid-term was coming up in her sophomore year, my granddaughter concluded she was not going to get anywhere with the coach and went to see him and explained she was leaving school. She explained she felt she needed to say her goodbyes to her teammates and wish them well as she chose to leave and get on with her life instead of wasting her time there. Four times during her conversation with him she asked to speak with the team and he told her he would take care of it. She carefully explained each time that she felt the need to tell them herself and she wanted to say her goodbyes to them. She politely requested to speak with all the girls after he was done speaking with them following the game. She had no intention of disparaging the coach. He finally told her she could do so. After the game where she sat on the bench the full time he told my granddaughter to wait in the locker room and he would come get her after announcing she had something to say to the team. She waited a long while but he never came or contacted her. She packed up her things after that and drove home late the night before Thanksgiving. When she arrived at 2:00 a.m. she went to her mother's side of the bed and sobbed long and hard. She announced she had quit school and felt terrible about giving up her scholarship.

My granddaughter saw and heard things done by her teammates and coach that were very disappointing and not honorable. She had to accept that she did not fit in and had no plan to compromise her Christian convictions. She saw Christian principles were sorely lacking in the team and

201

with the coach. She was very disillusioned by it all. It was not at all what she expected from the college she selected for furthering her education.

It appears her coach was intimidated by her as she was a self-thinker and he had made puppets of the rest. Strangely, he didn't seem grateful for such a talented team player. It seemed it was all about him. He chastised my granddaughter for having a black male friend and told her to stop. Again, he chastised her for going with two other girls to visit two girl friends in another college even though it was done on their free time and there were no rules against it. When he pointed out a poor play to another team member, it was done gently and sometimes with an arm around them. He was always harsh and blunt with my granddaughter. The coach and athletic director are considered close friends.

Leaving school was such an upsetting experience for my granddaughter that she broke out in a case of hives that it amazed the doctor who treated her as her skin is normally flawless. She still doesn't understand it all, but it hasn't shattered her faith in God. It did take a lot of courage. She is home now working part-time and taking classes at the local college as she waits to see what God has in store for her. Perhaps what she experienced will make her a better teacher and coach if that is what she becomes. It may well prove to be that what she experienced was not a lost cause at all. It took much courage for her to walk away. She knew it was costly financially and some people would be inclined to call her a quitter. She maintains she can't waste her energy and time on being concerned about negative thoughts of others. She makes it clear she needs to get on with her life. I congratulate her on moving out of the negative situation and with plans for better things through God. Her quitting midyear went through the high school where she graduated, through town and many places like a firestorm. It was a huge shock. When people understood, she received many positive comments. It took much more nobility for her to walk away from a bad situation than to stay in it to collect money in getting a college education. That is not a quitter. It is an overcomer. The understanding I empirically gained from my parents regarding overcoming even seemingly insurmountable adversities become obvious as they were passed on to my children and theirs. Though there are others in my family not included, the story of my granddaughter featured in this book is exemplary of children living what they learn. It is my desire that perusal of this book be of some benefit to every reader. Perhaps some have not had the advantage I did with parents who demonstrated their profound perseverance in overcoming.

Phyllis Bigelow

LaVergne, TN USA
16 December 2009

167123LV00002B/21/P